cousin camp

Books by Susan Alexander Yates

*And Then I Had Kids:
Encouragement for Mothers of Young Children*

And Then I Had Teenagers:
Encouragement for Parents of Teens and Preteens

31 Days of Prayer for My Teen

*Risky Faith, Becoming Brave Enough to Trust the God
Who Is Bigger Than Your World*

*One Devotional: One Word, One Verse,
One Thought for 100 Days*

A House Full of Friends: How to Like the Ones You Love

Character Matters: Raising Kids with Values That Last with
John W. Yates (Also published as Raising Kids with Character That Lasts)

Marriage Questions Women Ask
with Gloria Gaither and Gigi Tchividjian

31 Days of Prayer for My Child with Allison Yates Gaskins

Tightening the Knot with Allison Yates Gaskins

Thanks, Mom, for Everything with Allison Yates Gaskins

Thanks, Dad, for Everything with Allison Yates Gaskins

Building a Home Full of Grace with John W. Yates

A Home Full of Grace (published in the UK)
with John Yates and family

Barbara and Susan's Guide to the Empty Nest
with Barbara Rainey

*title is in print

For further information on Susan's blog, speaking schedule,
and other books, go to susanalexanderyates.com

"To know Susan Yates is to know the definition of the word *intentional*. We have marveled for years at her determination and commitment to growing meaningful relationships with her many grandchildren. Do you long to be an influence with your grands? Do you wish your parents were more engaged with your children? This book is full of ideas for both generations. Susan's wisdom and experience are sure to guide you to develop intentional multigenerational relationships too."

Dennis and Barbara Rainey, cofounders of FamilyLife, DennisandBarbara.com, and EverThineHome; authors of many books; parents to six and grandparents to twenty-four

"Susan Yates is someone Mary Ann and I have looked to through the years for wise counsel and practical help as we've raised our children. We are so thrilled to have that same godly wisdom available now as we begin our grandparenting years!"

Bob Lepine, cohost of *FamilyLife Today*

"Another winner by Susan Yates! *Cousin Camp* is a treasure trove of wisdom, ideas, and practical helps for passing on a legacy of love and faith to those you love most. I am on it—planning a yearly gathering to bless and build our family based on this very inspiring book!"

Pam Farrel, international speaker, codirector of Love-Wise, and author of fifty books including the bestselling *Men Are Like Waffles, Women Are Like Spaghetti*

"Susan had my full attention the first time she mentioned her Cousin Camp. Intrigued by the idea, I was eager to hear why she did this, then how and what and where. I instantly knew it was something I would want for our own family someday. Now Susan is offering helpful answers to all those same questions and many more—shared in her encouraging, inspiring, and always entertaining style. So get ready to create lasting memories and closer relationships for your entire family."

Lisa Jacobson, Club31Women.com

"The best things in life are based on beautiful relationships—relationships in which you know you are loved and valued. This is why I love *Cousin Camp* and highly recommend it! Author Susan Yates brings families together by teaching how to host a cousins' camp or family reunion, demonstrating how to be the catalyst for deeper, better relationships in your family . . . and all while everyone is having a blast together! It's so natural and positive. There's only one Susan Yates! Learn from a pro! Get your copy today!"

Matt Jacobson, FaithfulMan.com; *Faithful Life* podcast

"Effective grandparenting is a grand love backed up with a grand plan. We need a strategy for developing heart connection with each grandchild individually and are in the best position for helping all of our grandkids developing it as a group. Holidays can't do that. They're too crazy and distracted. But Cousin Camp can. And Susan Yates is just the seasoned grandparent to show you how it's done. You're going to love this winsome woman's advice and love even more the impact you'll make in your grandkids' lives."

Dr. Tim Kimmel and Darcy Kimmel, coauthors of *Extreme Grandparenting: the Ride of Your Life*

"Susan Alexander Yates understands the value of building strong families. Abiding in the twenty-first century, many of us lead hectic lives resulting in superficial relationships. Most of us long to draw close to our families. Yet bringing the extended family together can be daunting. Overflowing with practical guidelines for organizing family camps and reunions, *Cousin Camp* is an excellent resource for families of all sizes, backgrounds and needs. Knowing Susan for forty-seven years, I have been blessed to learn from her as she journeyed the ups and downs of being a mother and grandmother. What she writes is authentic. She shares what she has lived. This well-organized, delightful, inspiring, and informative book is realistic and encouraging to anyone longing to draw nearer to family. It is with joy I recommend it."

Catherine Jacobs, mother, grandmother, speaker, author of *Pass the Legacy: 7 Keys for Grandparents Making a Difference*, and director of Pass the Legacy Ministry

"*Cousin Camp* casts a vision for extended family that goes beyond 'civil' holiday gatherings. With an abundance of practical insight, Susan Yates shows how each of us can be cultivators of beautiful closeness, loyalty, and special memories among our relatives. Whether or not you grew up with a tight-knit extended family, this book will give you an expansive view of what family can be and help you create it."

Jedd and Rachel Medefind, presidents of the Christian Alliance for Orphans and parents of five

"Susan makes all of her ideas so doable and keeps the focus so beautifully on building relationships with one another and with Christ."

Jodie Berndt, speaker and author of the *Praying the Scriptures for Your Children* book series

cousin camp

A Grandparent's Guide to Creating Fun, Faith, and Memories That Last

Susan Alexander Yates

Revell

a division of Baker Publishing Group
Grand Rapids, Michigan

Published by Revell
a division of Baker Publishing Group
PO Box 6287, Grand Rapids, MI 49516-6287
www.revellbooks.com

Printed in the United States of America

Library of Congress Cataloging-in-Publication Data
Names: Yates, Susan Alexander, author.
Title: Cousin camp : a practical guide to creating fun, faith, and memories that last / Susan Alexander Yates.
Description: Grand Rapids, Michigan : Revell, a division of Baker Publishing Group, [2020] | Includes bibliographical references.
Identifiers: LCCN 2019037115 | ISBN 9780800738204 (paperback)
Subjects: LCSH: Families—Religious life. | Families—Religious aspects—Christianity. | Family reunions.
Classification: LCC BV4526.3 .Y39 2020 | DDC 249—dc23
LC record available at https://lccn.loc.gov/2019037115

Some names and details have been changed to protect the privacy of the individuals involved.

The author is represented by the literary agency of Wolgemuth & Associates.

20 21 22 23 24 25 26   7 6 5 4 3 2 1

To my husband, John, my best friend for over fifty years.
Without you there would be no books!

And for our children and grandchildren, I pray:
"My spirit, who is on you, will not depart from you, and my words that I have put in your mouth will always be on your lips, on the lips of your children and on the lips of their descendants—from this time on and forever," says the LORD. (Isa. 59:21)

Contents

Contents

Acknowledgments

A book is never a solo job. It is watered, fertilized, and nurtured by many people. I have a wonderful group of friends who have prayed for this project. I won't name you all because I'd probably forget someone. But know that your prayers and your support have meant the world to me, especially the women at The Falls Church Anglican, my home church.

I am particularly grateful to Robert and Erik Wolgemuth, my agents. Robert published my first book, *And Then I Had Kids*, way back in '89, and he's been a great friend to me for many years. My editor at Revell, Vicki Crumpton, is also a longtime friend and has edited other Yates books. I love working with you, Vicki.

A special shout-out to my friend Amanda Neely, who rescued me during the edits and helped me organize and track changes. What a gift you have been.

I am thankful to many friends who let me use their stories. Some names have been changed for privacy reasons, but all of the stories are true.

Special love and thanks to my children: Allison and Will Gaskins, Alysia and John Yates, Christy and Chris Yates, Susy and Scott Anderson, and Libby and McLean Wilson.

And to your children, our grandchildren, without whom this book never would have happened! Callie, Will, Tucker, Graham, and Davey Gaskins; Sylvia, Isabel, Jack, and Alexander Yates; Tobin, Cashel, Linden, and Saylor Yates; Grey, Mac, Mimi, Yates, and Fitz Wilson; Blaine, Hayes, and Sloan Anderson. Thank you for the joy you have brought to me ("Ghee") and "Poppy."

Most of all I am so blessed to be married to a very good man. Thank you, honey, for your prayers for me and our family for all these years. We had no clue what we were getting into in 1969! Thanks be to our faithful Lord.

He who calls you is faithful; he will surely do it.
(1 Thess. 5:24 ESV)

Introduction

I never ever imagined my life would turn out the way it did. I was the strong-willed eldest of four kids and really did not like my siblings. When my mother gave birth to a second boy, I was so mad I would not speak to her for three days. I had wanted a sister. (Later I did get a sister!) As a youngster I much preferred playing football with the neighborhood boys to babysitting. I once shot a twelve-year-old boy with a BB gun just because he made me mad. Thrilling adventures included sneaking up to a house, ringing the doorbell, and running, then returning to do it again. One day I cut my brother's hair off just because I didn't like it.

My parents were people with a strong faith, so our family went to church. It was not negotiable. I thought it was boring and slept through many services. I would never have imagined *wanting* to go to church. As a teen I was not in the "cool crowd." I didn't think too much about marriage and family. Instead I wanted to go to law school and run for congress or even vice president. In those days, women were not encouraged to do this.

So, what happened?

God has a sense of humor. I married a man who was in seminary. He became a minister, and we've been serving in churches for fifty years. We had five children in seven years, including a set of twins. All of our kids are married, and we have twenty-one grandchildren. And along the way I began to write books and speak on the family.

Gradually, God changed my heart. During my college years I realized that my faith was an "inherited faith" of my parents and my culture. It was not a personal faith. The summer before my junior year I asked Christ to come into my life. Although I had many questions, I also had a hunger that was new to me, a hunger to get to know God and His Son, Jesus. He began to give me a passion for young people and for families. Both my husband, John, and I had the blessing of being raised in strong families. Our parents weren't perfect. None are. But they provided us with a strong foundation for family life. And the older I get, the more I appreciate them. No one chooses the family into which they are born. That's God's choice. Early in our marriage we realized that we had been given a gift—the heritage of wise parents. And we had an opportunity to steward this gift to encourage others in growing strong families.

Our growth has been gradual, changing with each season of life. In the early years we were merely trying to survive. Then within eight years our five kids got married, so now we say we have ten kids (spouses included). Grandchildren began to arrive. Our two greatest desires have always been that our kids would love the Lord and love each other. This is the legacy we want to hand down to our grandchildren and their kids and the generations to come.

We know a legacy doesn't just "happen." We have to be *intentional*.

That's what this book is about.

Many things go into building a legacy. This book is just one small piece of a much larger puzzle.

It's also helpful to think of your family as one large puzzle. There are many distinct pieces all having to fit together in order to make one beautiful picture. The artist knows what the finished product will look like. And it is beautiful to its creator.

Years ago, we began hosting an annual "Cousin Camp." We wanted our grandchildren from five different families living in different places to know one another. And we wanted focused time with them without their parents. You have to be age four to come to our camp. We started with five children, and the past three summers all twenty-one of our grandchildren have attended. Last summer we celebrated our eleventh year of camp.

We've made lots of mistakes, shed tears, laughed uproariously, thrown out plans, separated quarreling kids, cheered when kindness overcame selfishness, and fallen into bed exhausted, but above all we've had a blast. Seeing two girl cousins who used to fight like cats now snuggling on our bedroom floor in sleeping bags, giggling together, makes it all worth it.

Over the years we've also hosted extended family reunions. Camp is only one piece of building a close family. There are many others. My hope is that this book will encourage you to be *intentional* in one way as you put together your own family puzzle.

There are three sections to this book. Each is important. So often when planning an event, we want to go straight to the daily schedule to glean ideas for crafts, for Bible study, for meals. However, it is most important to consider the *why* of what you want to do first. There are principles that need to undergird the event in order for it to succeed and have lasting value. The first part of this book deals with these principles. Part 2 focuses on the "nuts and bolts" of Cousin Camp. You can apply many of these ideas to all types of family gatherings. Part 3 will give you creative ideas for all sorts of family reunions. The final chapter provides the key ingredient that makes everything work: prayer.

Don't skip part 1!

part 1

Why Have a Cousin Camp or Family Reunion?

one

Family Is God's Idea

I have always had great fun imagining what it must have been like in heaven when God created the world, and particularly what the conversation must have been like between the Father and the Son. Imagine their delight as their amazing creative powers brought into being the day and the night, the sun and the moon, the earth and the great seas, and the unbelievably diverse assortment of animals and creatures. It makes me laugh to imagine them thinking up a rhinoceros or a flat-footed platypus.

However, the most astonishing thing about creation is that God created us human beings to be His children. There was nothing incomplete about God's life, and the fellowship in heaven between the Holy Trinity and the angelic hosts must have been beautiful beyond our comprehension.

So *why* did the Father, Son, and Holy Spirit make man and woman? I like to think that perhaps they were lonely. They wanted a family. Or maybe they simply wanted to share the joy of relationships by creating others with whom to interact. They wanted something more than angels, who are not made in God's image but who are "ministering spirits sent to serve those who will inherit

19

salvation" (Heb. 1:14). They wanted a man and woman, made in God's image, to enjoy God's creation, to cultivate it, and to live in perfect fellowship with each other and with them.

The point here is that God created family, and He says it is good. We aren't meant to be alone. *Family* has a broad meaning. We usually think of family as a dad, mom, and kids. But throughout both the Old and New Testaments we see family described as large tribes, small units, and particularly the family of the church. A family might include singles as well as married people, young people, and old people. God knows that we are not meant to be alone. We need one another. The big concept here can be summarized in a single word: *together*.

Our God is a visionary. He's passionate about generations and who is to come. Isaiah declares,

> "As for me, this is my covenant with them," says the LORD. "My spirit, who is on you, will not depart from you, and my words that I have put in your mouth will always be on your lips, on the lips of your children and on the lips of their descendants—from this time on and forever," says the LORD. (Isa. 59:21)

I believe God wants us to be passionate about future generations and about what is most important for each one.

When Christ was asked, "Which is the greatest commandment in the law?" He replied, "'Love the Lord your God with all your heart and with all your soul and with all your mind.' This is the first and greatest commandment. And the second is like it: 'Love your neighbor as yourself'" (Matt. 22:36–39).

Our family members are our closest neighbors. Yes, they can sometimes be the hardest to love. But if it were easy, we wouldn't need God's help. He knows we are weak, and He's given us forgiveness through His Son and the power to change through His Holy Spirit.

When we think about God creating family, we think not only about our own immediate family but also about future generations to come.

As parents and grandparents, we want to see our future generations become people who love Christ and each other.

How do we help this happen?

Families Are Messy

Sometimes I picture a group of children telling the creation story. Eventually they'd also have to talk about Adam and Eve's disobedience. Of their wanting to have the one thing they couldn't. Of realizing their nakedness. (Now, that would be a hilarious children's conversation.)

The kids would remind us that God never gave up on His family. Ultimately, because He loved us so much, He gave His own Son so that we might be forgiven of our inherent selfishness (sin) and restored into relationship with Him.

Jesus Christ died for us—in the middle of our mess.

There is no perfect family. We are all a mess to some degree. Instagram, Facebook, and Pinterest are only images. Behind every perfect photo is a self-centered person. One who has used ugly words, done awful things, hurt other people, and even discovered they didn't like themselves very much.

It's easy to think, *But my family is a mess! My home of origin was strange. My kids fight, my marriage is shaky, our parents don't understand or support us, and our extended family is very dysfunctional.* Or we think, *I'm a single parent or a single person. Is there a place and a vision for me? How can I even begin to think about shaping the next generation?*

It helps to remember that God is not shocked by your situation, by your wounds, or by your history. He's seen it all. And there's nothing He can't forgive, nothing He can't change, and no one He can't heal. As Luke says, "For nothing will be impossible with God" (Luke 1:37 ESV).

So, no matter where you come from or your current marital status, you can be the first generation of a healthy family.

How can this happen?

Well, to begin with, you have to become *intentional*. And you have to become *dependent* on the Lord.

Building a strong family and shaping future generations will not just happen. It begins with prayer and planning. Strong families grow when bonds are developed through the nurturing of relationships.

This book is about one way to influence future generations for good: hosting a Cousin Camp or another type of family reunion.

It is important to understand several ingredients before we make a plan.

Let Grace Rule

You may have a difficult relationship with your daughter-in-law. You wonder if she likes you. Or your son may be in a hard place, and you feel him withdrawing from you and the family. Cousins may not have much in common or may even dislike each other.

Decide now to set aside your assumptions and choose to let grace rule. This may involve choosing kind words (Prov. 16:24) or remaining silent when offended (Prov. 17:28).

Solomon said it this way: "A person's wisdom yields patience; it is to one's glory to overlook an offense. . . . Gracious words are a honeycomb, sweet to the soul and healing to the bones" (Prov. 19:11; 16:24).

Be Quick to Forgive

I can't tell you how many times I've had to go to my husband and to my children (and friends too) and say, "I need to ask you to forgive me for _____. Will you please forgive me?"

I can't remember a single time I've *felt* like doing this. I'd much rather chime in with, "But if you had or hadn't . . ."

We go to one another to ask for forgiveness not out of feelings but out of obedience. God has called us to do this. Feelings and trust take time to be healed and restored, often a long time. But asking for forgiveness opens the door to allow healing to take place and trust to begin to be rebuilt. Asking for forgiveness is different than saying, "I'm sorry."

Saying, "I'm sorry" doesn't demand a response. We might say, "I'm sorry" for backing into the telephone pole and denting the car, for breaking a lamp, for forgetting to do what was asked. Our child might say, "Sorry," dripping with sarcasm as she stomps out of the room. Sometimes, "I'm sorry" is appropriate, but when we wound another person, we need to confess and ask for forgiveness.

We are also to forgive others, even if they don't ask for forgiveness. When Jesus taught the disciples how to pray (the Lord's Prayer) he told them to say, "Forgive us our debts, as we also have forgiven our debtors" (Matt. 6:12). *Debts* translates into sins. Note: Jesus doesn't say *if* that person who hurt you asks to be forgiven, then forgive. Instead, He calls us to take the initiative. To forgive anyway. No matter what. Forgiveness does not automatically bring good feelings or restore trust. These take time and the help of the Holy Spirit, and often good counsel.

I believe that forgiveness is the most important ingredient in the family. God willing, we are raising future husbands and wives. How will they know how to forgive their own spouses and family members if we don't practice this in our homes?

Assume the Best

You'd like to host a Cousin Camp or a family gathering; however, there's one family with whom you aren't close or with whom there are unresolved issues. Should you invite them? Yes.

We must be *intentional* in assuming the best. That person may be struggling with something that has nothing to do with you. Don't take it personally. And don't assume the worst. Assume they need your love and that this opportunity may bring healing to their wounds. Extend grace. If appropriate, have other family members reach out to them.

I know of two adult siblings who were at odds with one another. Both had children. A family gathering wasn't particularly appealing to them, but because they wanted their children to know each other, they came. As the cousins built friendships, the adults began to experience healing in their relationships. Sometimes it takes the next generation to lead the elders.

A Cousin Camp is not the time to confront issues. It's a time to celebrate the good in what we do have. Choose another time and place during the year to deal with difficult issues. Paul reminds us, "If it is possible, as far as it depends on you, live at peace with everyone" (Rom. 12:18).

Avoid the Comparison Trap

One of the challenges for us as we try to raise our families and to plan an event is that we look at *that other* family, which seems so perfect. Of course, the word *seems* is key.

There is no perfect family. No one has it all together. Just like Adam and Eve, we want what we don't have. Looking at another family can either inspire us or discourage us. It depends on our lenses.

I wear contacts, and each of my eyes needs a different contact lens. It's important that I get the correct lens in the appropriate eye, otherwise my vision will be distorted. My eyes won't see clearly. I will become discouraged and grouchy. I'll stumble around. I'll get tired.

We need to look at other families not through lenses of jealousy and envy but with eyes of grace and thanksgiving.

Choose to learn from other families. Adopt what they have done that might work for your family. Leave out what does not relate to your family.

Cultivate Your Vision

What is your vision for your family? Think about your dreams, wishes, and hopes. What matters most to you? With this in mind, ask yourself, *What is my vision for a Cousin Camp? What do I most want to see happen? What do I hope the results will be?* For example:

- I want my family members to really know one another.
- I long for reconciliation within my family.
- I want my family to know Christ.
- I hope the next generations of my family will support one another when I am no longer there.

John and I have a very simple vision for our family. We long for each member to love the Lord with all their heart, mind, and soul and to love and care for each other (see Matt. 22:37–39).

We pray that our grandchildren will come to know Jesus at an early age and determine to walk with Him all their lives. We pray that if it's God's will they marry, they marry believers. And we are praying for the parents who are raising their future spouses, just as we did for our own children. I hoped there was someone out there praying for me as I raised my kids. I needed those prayers! We pray that our grandchildren will develop friendships with each other and support one another always. We pray that those blessed financially would support other cousins in need.

It's a fun project to discuss these questions together as a couple. If you are a single parent, join with another single parent or with another couple in your same season of life and dream about this together.

Questions to Consider

1. When you look at your family members, what are you thankful for?

2. What would you like God to do in the coming years in your family? (Be as specific as possible.)

3. How can you encourage the strengths and gifts of different family members?

two

A Different Way to Plan

When we think of planning an event, we typically begin with the program. Where should we go? What should we do? What should we eat? Will we have a theme? What about decorations? We design a wonderful party or reunion that most people enjoy—but then it's over.

When planning a family gathering, we need to ask, While the event might have good results, will they last? What if we carefully considered the goals of our event and the needs of the people attending? Would this enable a fun event to have more of a long-term impact?

A New Paradigm

When John and I were young, we planned events just to have a good event. But then we sat at the feet of Chuck Miller, a wise pastor, and his wife, Cathy. They gave us a different paradigm.

They taught us that the program should flow from the needs and goals of the people involved. To help us begin to think in this way, we first wrote down the names of those attending. Then we made three columns on the page, titled Needs, Goals, and Program (who will do what). Under Needs we consider five areas of growth: emotional, social, physical, spiritual, and mental. Below is an example of how our planning chart looks. (See "Worksheet for Children's Needs" on page 136 in the appendix for a blank form.)

You can make changes throughout camp as needed. After camp is over, it is fun to look back at this to notice what worked (or didn't) and to jot down notes for next year. The purpose of this exercise is to establish a new way of thinking, not to see perfection.

We consider character traits we want to encourage—kindness, sharing, affirming. And we consider each child's unique gifts. Is one musical, another competitive, another compassionate? Solomon advises us, "Be sure you know the condition of your flocks, give careful attention to your herds" (Prov. 27:23). I take this as a mandate to study my children and my grandchildren. I ask God how He has packaged each one, and I ask Him to lead me in knowing ways to foster their individual gifts.

This approach to planning might sound a little overwhelming. And it is at first. But as you continue to do this, it will become second nature to think in this way. It also helps us to keep the *why* question in mind. *Why* are we doing this particular thing?

John and I have used this paradigm throughout more than fifty years of ministry and in raising all of our kids. It has been a huge help in both arenas and has enabled us to see God answer specific prayers. Using this method is more likely to bring about long-term results from your event.

When we start planning camp each year, we follow this process. Why? Because needs change. Our grandchildren are growing. So are we. The number of kids coming to camp changes year to year too. We approach each camp with a fresh perspective. But this doesn't mean we create an entirely new schedule every year. Kids like routine. They like to know what to expect.

Name	Needs	Goals	Program
Sloan (age 4)	*Emotional:* First year at camp, will be shy, needs to be pulled in.	Learn the names of all her first cousins.	Ghee has a photo of everyone posted with names.
	Social: Feel she has a special friend.	She and Saylor (also age 4) begin to bond.	Ghee makes a bed on the floor in their bedroom for Sloan and Saylor to sleep together.
	Physical: She will get tired.	She goes to her "floor bed" in Ghee and Poppy's room for "rest time" in case she falls asleep.	Ghee "rests" on her bed so she can keep girls from talking during "rest time."
	Spiritual: Ask Christ into her life if she wants to.	Be assured she knows Him.	Her cousins share during Bible study how/when they asked Christ into their lives.
	Mental: No particular need here.		
Davey (age 10)	*Emotional:* Feel he is special in view of being the youngest of five.	Has good guy cousin time apart from his siblings.	We put him on teams without some siblings and provide opportunities for him and cousin Jack to be together.
	Social: Begin to care for others.	His relationships with younger cousins begin to grow.	Give him specific small things to do with younger cousins, i.e. help them with soccer.
	Physical: Needs to expend energy.	He is tired by the day's end.	Ask him to organize a soccer game (Poppy).
	Spiritual: Be attracted to Scripture.	He develops an interest in the Word of God.	Poppy asks him to read Scripture during Bible study.
	Mental: Unclear.		

Linden (age 6)	Emotional: Needs to be separated from a brother.	We avoid some sibling conflict.	We are *alert* to keeping them apart.
	Social: Want her to bond with cousin Grey.	These two same-age girls begin a friendship.	Grey and Linden sleep together. We give them creative things to do—just the two of them.
	Physical: Very athletic, loves horses.	Encourage her love of horses.	Poppy puts her in charge of cleaning stalls, getting horses ready (with Poppy's help).
	Spiritual: Reaffirm her decision for Christ.	She is confident in her testimony.	Let her be one to share her testimony from her journal during Bible study.
	Mental: Naturally smart, a leader.	Encourage her to read and lead so she grows in confidence.	Give her appropriate opportunities to be in charge.
Tobin (age 13)	Emotional: Realize he can be influential.	Develop his leadership gifts.	Make him team captain.
	Social: Engage with others (not his siblings).	He takes initiative with others.	Make sure he is spending time with his assigned buddy—suggest how.
	Physical: Very athletic.	Use his natural ability to encourage, not merely compete.	Poppy asks him to develop the brackets for the ping pong tournament and to organize it.
	Spiritual: To be ready for the next step in spiritual growth with same-age cousins.	He will want to become a man of God.	Poppy spends thirty minutes alone with older grandkids to share his own habit of praying and reading the Bible in the morning. He shows them old journals and notes from when he has prayed for them specifically.
	Mental: Be challenged to grow.	Express what he's learning with others.	Poppy asks him about books he is reading and his favorite subjects.

A few years into camp I worried that the kids would become bored with the same schedule, so I asked my older "camp mentor" Judy what she thought. "No," she replied. "Keep the main blocks and just change up and introduce new little things. This gives them security—and saves you a lot of time." Of course, if something "flopped" last year, we throw that out, but generally the blocks in each day remain the same.

Working Together as a Couple

Every marriage is different. You and your spouse are different people with different gifts. You both have different time constraints and obligations. When we began Cousin Camp, John was the senior pastor of a large church. I was speaking and writing, but my schedule was not as packed as his was. So, for us, the primary planning has fallen on my shoulders. I am better at planning events and considering the needs of little people. John has great wisdom and is levelheaded, so he brings those gifts to the process. John does much of the "upfront" work, leading activities as much as possible during camp. He usually chooses our camp verse and the focus of our Bible studies.

We both get tired and frustrated throughout camp. I remember a year when one grandson was being difficult, so I asked John to deal with him. I knew he would be better in that situation. We've both learned to say, "I'm about to lose it; I need you to take over." We determine not to judge who is working harder or doing more. We remind ourselves that we are on the same team together, balancing one another and covering for each other. And we expect to be fully exhausted by the time the parents arrive on the last day!

Your husband may be the better planner and the game leader. You may handle the down times better. The principle here is to recognize that you are packaged differently and you can use your gifts to complete one another, not compete with each other. Consider who has more time to do the planning and the gathering of stuff (food, supplies, etc.). The more you do ahead, the easier it will be on you.

And as you plan together, pray together. This makes a wonderful difference (see "'Praying Together for Your Children Builds Your Marriage' Blog Post" on page 137 in the appendix).

Enlist a Prayer Team

Several weeks before camp, I ask a small group of good friends to pray for us. Here are the kinds of things to ask for prayer for:

- No family emergencies that would keep anyone from coming
- Safety at camp, with no accidents or illnesses
- Acceptable weather
- That certain kids would bond with each other
- Patience for the grandparents, that you'd give each other grace and overlook picky marital irritations
- That there would be lots of laughter instead of frustration
- That you'd be able to encourage your grandkids' spiritual growth
- That any who have not personally received Christ's salvation would come to know Him

Our prayer requests change year to year as needs change, but it helps us so much to know that friends have our back and are on their knees praying for us.

We can't do this alone. I think of Moses, who had Aaron and Hur to hold up his arms during battle. He was too weak himself. And I remember the story of Paul, who spent his time in jail praying for his friends in Philippi and other places. How we need one another in the body of Christ. We can't do things as important as family reunions without this kind of support!

32

Maintain a Clear Vision

In our planning, we continually go back to our main vision: *That our grandchildren would love the Lord and love each other.* Keeping this simple goal in front of us enables us not to feel overwhelmed or to get distracted as we get into the details of planning. Every now and then we ask ourselves, *How will this activity or decision accomplish our goals and foster our vision?*

However, also keep in mind that everything doesn't have to be spiritual or serious. One of our goals is simply to laugh. So we always have a huge whipped cream "fight."

The first year we did this, I used shaving cream. Bad idea. It stung and tasted gross. The next year with nineteen grands, we switched to the sweet stuff. The kids love this, and also love squirting one another with the hose to rinse out sticky hair afterward. I even got a discount at the grocery store when I bought twenty-four cans of whipped cream! (Yes, always have spares, in case one can doesn't work.) For those who don't want sticky hair, give them shower caps. The ones you get for free at hotels are perfect!

Be Patient and Think Long-Term

In your planning, it's important to keep a long-range perspective. Ask, How can a specific activity have a lasting impact in encouraging our kids' faith or in encouraging their relationships? Ten years from now, will *this* (whatever "this" is) have made a difference?

We may not see results right away. A grandson might give his life to Christ, and yet it doesn't seem to make any difference. Two cousins you had hoped would be friends seem to argue more than they enjoy one another. An older granddaughter you had hoped would be sensitive to younger cousins is only interested in herself.

When things like these happen, I remember when John and I had young children. The hardest things to teach can be politeness, sharing, obedience, and caring. Sometimes, no matter how hard you try, children are still rude, want what they want when they want it, and don't share with a sibling. Parenting (and grandparenting) can be exhausting, and we wonder if we are failing. Will they ever get it? Yes, but not usually *now*.

So we keep training and trust that in God's time these kids will grow into maturity. Even when we can't see results right away.

In the winter, nature can look gray and bleak. Color and beauty can be in short supply after a long, cold, wet stretch, and we wonder if blue skies and color will return. Yet during this stagnant time God is at work. Underneath the ground He is preparing marvelous plants that will burst forth at just the right time. It may seem barren, but God is working while we are waiting. The same thing is true with our kids. *He is working while we are waiting.* Paul says it this way: "[Be] confident of this, that he who began a good work in you will carry it on to completion until the day of Christ Jesus" (Phil. 1:6).

Over the years, one of the things that has been so special for John and me has been watching our grandchildren grow up. It has been nothing short of marvelous.

For eleven years we have hosted Cousin Camp. Each year the older kids have taken on more responsibility during our time together. We are very intentional in having them do more. *Why?* Because we want them to learn how to be responsible, to carry out a task, and to serve others. Even though camp is just a few days long, it can still have an impact on their character development. One day we won't be here and, God willing, our grandkids will be parents themselves.

At our first camp, we had five cousins: three siblings and two cousins from two different families. Callie, our eldest grandchild, was ten, and the others were eight, five, five, and four. Callie is the only girl in her family with four little brothers. When she was young, she really didn't like her brothers. This is pretty normal; my young children didn't like each other very much either.

A few years ago, Callie turned seventeen. At the close of camp, we asked her to write her reflections about Cousin Camp.

"Short-term sleep deprivation—long-term love!"

I'd say I'm exhausted, but that would be a gross understatement. Exhausted, ecstatic, wistful . . . the list goes on. I'm less than twelve hours out from Cousin Camp 2016, and at this point I don't really know what hit me. I spent the weekend enveloped in chaos and occasionally sweet cousin cuddles, but in my tired state everything seems like a blur.

Yes, we did sit through morning quiet times and afternoon rest periods, but those brief instances of "calm" are overshadowed by the pandemonium of the rest of the weekend. Traditions such as receiving fun T-shirts made by our uncle, a trip to the vineyard for a picnic, and the induction of the new campers into the "Band of Cousins" were complemented by the introduction of teams ("for cooperation, not competition" as Ghee insisted . . . but to no avail!) and the highlight of the weekend: a giant obstacle course.

However, all of these planned activities, while fun, were not the highlight of Cousin Camp—they never are. The real highlights were the impromptu things: precariously stacking five Eno hammocks on top of one another, catching what is probably the second largest fish to ever come out of the pond, one of the boys insisting that watermelon is a Fruit of the Spirit, and guacamole-making competitions, among other things. These delightful times serve as catalysts for what I hope will be lifelong relationships between us cousins.

As I lay in bed on Sunday night trying not to wake the cousin asleep next to me, I couldn't help but think back on the past nine years of Cousin Camp. From the "fab five" in 2008 to the "terrific twenty-one" this year, camp has always been a highlight of my summer. Although I may occasionally complain about my role, I am so lucky to be the eldest. I've been able to watch all twenty of these little ones grow up, finally make it to age four, attend their first Cousin Camp, and end the weekend excited for the next year. These sweet ones are a huge part of my life, and I can only hope that as I head off to Charlottesville in the fall, I won't be leaving this behind. I don't want to be a distant memory for the youngest two, but someone who is as important to them as they have been to me. I'm so grateful that my grandparents instituted the tradition of Cousin Camp, because it is the perfect way to ensure that there will always be a reason for us to get together, year after year.

Questions to Consider

1. List the names of your grandchildren. Ask yourself, *How has God packaged each one?* (You can also ask their parents for insights.) Beside the name of each child, list:

   A. What you notice about their nature (sensitive, leadership gifts, etc.)

   B. What their interests are (sports, technology, art, etc.)

2. What different gifts do you and your spouse bring to the table? How might these gifts work out in planning a camp? (If you are single, do this with a camp cohost.)

3. What is your vision for your camp? Discuss and write your ideas down. You may want to edit it later, and that's fine.

three

Balancing Realistic Expectations with Surprises

In planning a camp, we bring different expectations to the table. Expectations like fun, hugs, love, laughter, joy, instant connections, meaningful conversations, steps of faith, sweet times of prayer, scintillating Bible studies, healthy meals, sound sleep, cooperation, thoughtfulness, appreciation—oops, not so fast!

Instead, reality might be a child whose feelings get hurt, another who doesn't want to play the group game, or two brothers who have to be separated.

While we always dream our camp will be a complete blast, we are still a family of sinners, and we are not perfect. Remembering this helps us to formulate some realistic expectations and enables us not to focus on the disappointments but instead to laugh when they occur and move on.

Before our first camp, I worked hard to get the house clean. I wanted my kids to be impressed when they dropped their kids off for camp. My house was organized and neat. I put flowers in different rooms, even the bathrooms! My friend Elaine came over to see my "perfect" house. I knew she would appreciate it too. It felt so good. Then the families arrived. Kids were all over the house. Sleeping bags and backpacks were dumped everywhere; dirt was tracked inside. No one noticed anything. Not even my flowers. Soon the house was trashed.

I called Elaine.

"Please come back over. I need you to see this!" I exclaimed. "I need a girlfriend who understands."

We both gasped as we looked in every room.

I realized that I had to give up my expectation of a neat house for these days. Was it more important that I nagged the kids and exhausted myself picking up or that we had a good time? In the long run, what would matter most? Clean house or happy kids?

I had to make a choice. I chose happy kids and tried hard not to nag or pick up after them. And since then I have *not* cleaned my house just before camp!

Another expectation I had was that John and I would have significant conversations with each grandchild. Ha. The kids were more excited to see one another. Each year, as our numbers grew, we had fewer and fewer meaningful conversations. There were too many kids. I realized that these kinds of conversations were not a realistic expectation nor should they even be a goal. The goal was for the cousins to bond with each other. There would be other times during the year for us to bond with individual grandchildren, but camp is not primarily about us. It is about them and their relationships with each other.

Simply adjusting our expectations enables us to enjoy camp.

Wonderful Surprises

One of the surprises for us has been that the kids behave better for us than they do for their parents. Positive cousin peer pressure plays a role in this. There is not much whining.

For example, like his cousins before him, Davey came for his first camp when he was four. He learned to fill his own water bottle when he was thirsty. He rarely needed his blanket. He joined in fixing things for himself because the bigger guys were doing it too. I can't remember him whining—until his mother showed up at the end of camp. When she walked in the door, he whined, needed his blanket, had to curl up in her lap, and wanted *her* to get him a drink of water!

"Davey," I said, "show your mommy how you have learned to find and fill your own water bottle. You don't need her to get your water anymore. You are a big camper now!"

Grandparents can get away with things parents can't. We don't experience the "eye roll" as much as parents do. The kids are more polite to their grandparents. We can ask teens specific questions without receiving an exasperated, "Oh, Mom . . ." response. Sometimes we even get more out of our grandkids than their parents do! It's a wonderful blessing for this season.

Occasionally it's the kids who come up with the surprises. I am not a great cook, but several of my grands are. Influenced by all the cooking shows, they created a guacamole "cook-off" contest with three different teams. It was hysterical—and it was not in our plans. It was their idea.

Balancing High Hopes and Realistic Expectations

There's an inherent tension between high hopes, realistic expectations, and the willingness to change course. It's true in life, and it's true at camp. Expectations come in different forms.

Logistical Expectations

You may already be saying, "The Yateses have a little farm. We don't. How can we have Cousin Camp?" You can have a camp anywhere. It will just look different (we'll discuss this more in chapter 5). Our farm is not fancy. We pack kids in; they sleep on couches, on floors, and even in closets. And we've pitched a tent. Also, our neighbors share their rooms with us when the whole family comes in for Family Camp.

"What about the expenses? How can we afford to do this?" You don't need to spend a lot on things. We keep it simple. Our biggest expense has become food to feed all these kids. Most of you will not have twenty-one grands to feed! We keep the menu simple: mac 'n' cheese, chicken tenders, hamburgers, hot dogs, and lots of sandwiches and salads. For us, camp is not about the food.

Clean kids, baths? Not happening every day. The kids get dirty, most hair does not get washed, and if teeth get brushed (often with a buddy's help) it's an accomplishment!

We let the parents know ahead of time that we will not have electronic devices at camp for anyone under age sixteen. Our goal is to focus on each other, not on a screen. The older kids use their devices on a very limited basis, with permission, mainly to help us make camp movies and take photos.

Expectations of Ourselves

John and I began with high expectations of ourselves. We soon realized we could not measure up. We get tired and grumpy. We have to grant each other extra grace. We work hard to choose laughter instead of frustration. If one of us has a hard time with a child, we ask the other to step in. We expect to be completely exhausted by the end of camp. That's realistic.

It can be easy to fall into self-condemnation because you aren't measuring up to your own expectations. This is a trap of the enemy. Paul tells us in Romans 8:1, "Therefore, there is now no condemnation for those who are in Christ Jesus." God loves us. He forgives us. We are to walk in His grace and power, not in our own strength. Condemnation is from the enemy and might sound like this: *You are a lousy grandparent, a crummy wife.* These phrases are general condemnations from Satan. The Holy Spirit, on the other hand, convicts specifically. *Susan, you should not have spoken to John like that, and you need to ask his forgiveness.* This is a specific conviction. It helps to recognize this distinction between condemnation and conviction. If it is a general condemnation, tell the enemy to flee and remind yourself of God's love. Do not wallow in the condemnation. If it's a specific conviction, ask for forgiveness.

I love David's words in Psalm 103:13–14: "As a father has compassion on his children, so the LORD has compassion on those who fear him; for he knows how we are formed, he remembers that we are dust." What a relief. Too often we put expectations on ourselves that God never intended us to have.

Expectations of the Cousins

You may have specific expectations for the cousins. Be prepared to adjust your plans and be creative. I remember the year I had high hopes for two boy cousins who barely knew each other to bond. They were both eight years old. One of them was not the least bit interested in the other, and he chose instead to hang out with the older boys, ignoring this cousin who really wanted to spend time with him. Things didn't go well that year. But the next year we created some options that both of these boys were interested in, and they spent a lot of time together. It took time to nurture a relationship and a lot of prayer and creativity. As seeds do not mature and spring forth instantly, so it takes a while for relationships to develop. You are planting seeds, and you may have to wait to see results.

Know When to Let Go

One year, when the kids were small, we planned to learn two new songs to perform for the parents when they arrived, but we had to throw that out. We were lousy singers. However, things change,

43

and by our eleventh camp we had some budding musicians. I was thrilled when three of the older kids agreed to write a song (grandmother pressure) for our closing ceremony. It took eleven years to happen! (And it was precious.) Still, we'll never be on tour.

There's one big expectation we all need to let go of, over and over. It's the expectation of being appreciated. We want our adult children to appreciate us, and we want our grandchildren to appreciate us. We long to hear, "Thank you so much. I had the best time ever at camp," "Thanks for all your hard work," "Thank you for getting the goody bags and treats and crafts," and so on. If we count on being appreciated, we will be disappointed. I remember one awful seven-hour car ride with my parents. I had all five kids with me, including six-month-old twins who screamed most of the trip. I imagine my dad was tempted to stop the car and let us out! It was a disaster. Do I remember thanking my parents? No. But today I appreciate them. There's a Scripture that says, "Her children [you can add grandchildren] arise and call her blessed" (Prov. 31:28). I like to chuckle and add, ". . . not for at least twenty years." We are building for the future and it's unrealistic to expect to be appreciated now. Instead, find a friend who will appreciate your efforts and praise your hard work!

We make lots of plans for camp. And then things don't go as we'd hoped. How do we respond?

When do we let go of control, and when do we hold fast? We let go of the schedule and the events. We hold fast when things relate to character.

Once we began to have both teens and young children at camp, we established two different bedtimes. The under-nines went to bed early, while the over-nines stayed up. We planned a special night time of sharing around the outdoor fireplace for the older kids. However, these kids had invented an outdoor hide-and-seek game called "man hunt" that they wanted to play. It seemed smarter to drop our plan and go with their game. It was a place where we should be flexible.

Cousin Camp Song

Written and performed by Isabel, Graham, Cashel, and Sylvie
Parody on "Riptide" by Vance Joy

I was scared of Charlie and deer ticks
I was scared of riding horses oh I don't want to get bit
All my cousins have already been
It's finally the year that I join in

Ahh-ooooh-ooh (2x)

Young kids running down to the slip 'n' slide
Carried away by the soapy slime
How 'bout another whipped cream fight

I love it when we go on a car ride
Picking berries in sunshine
Pies and tarts from cooking class

There's a contest that I think I'll win
Pinging pong and hula-hoop and Father's Day skits
Horses walking by the barn
Trail rides show Poppy what we've learned

Ahh-oooooh-ooooh-oooh (2x) fun
And it's gonna be fun

Old kids staying up past midnight
Sitting out in the starlight
Card games, fishing, and saying good night

Cousins gathered round the fire
Making s'mores and talking
About the world we know well

Ahh-ooooh-ooooh-oooh (2x)
And it has been so fun!

However, when two of the girl cousins left a third girl cousin out and told her she couldn't play with them, they were just being "mean girls." Not kind at all. Kindness is a character trait, so I had a talk with the girls, explained why it's important to be kind, and insisted they play together.

Schedules (plans) are not sacred; character matters. It helps to ask yourself, *Does this have to do with character, or is this something with which we can be flexible?*

God's Expectations?

What does God expect? That is a loaded question! I believe He expects us to depend upon Him. Yes, we are to love the Lord with all our heart, mind, and soul, and love our neighbor as ourselves, but we can't do that without God's help. Growing in our relationship with God involves becoming more dependent upon Him, not less.

He doesn't expect perfection or that we become the best grandparents ever. He doesn't expect a perfect Cousin Camp. God loves us simply because we belong to Him. Period.

I grew up with a dad who was both verbally and physically affectionate. I remember on many occasions he'd pull me into his lap and say, "Susan, I love you so much." "Why, Daddy?" I'd ask. "Just because you are mine," was his response. It wasn't because I'd been good. I was the strong-willed eldest of four kids and hard to raise. No, it was merely because I belonged to him. That's how our heavenly Father feels about you and me. He loves us not because we are good grandparents or run a successful camp, but simply because we belong to Him.

A Special Calling

As grandparents, most of us don't have the major responsibility for raising our grandkids. That's the parents' responsibility. For those of you who are raising your grandchildren, may God bless you, equip you, and give you friends to walk alongside you and to encourage you.

No matter what our personal situation is, we have an opportunity and a special calling: to pray for our grandchildren and for their parents.

God's story is that of generations. In both the Old and New Testaments, the word *generation* (or *generations, family,* or *families*) is mentioned at least 150 times. Think of all the Scriptures with long lists of genealogies. Why bother with all these family names we can't even pronounce? One reason is that God cares about our family lines. Notice the many heroes in Scripture who prayed for future generations. Moses gave God's commandments to the Israelites, saying that it was "so that you, your children and their children after them may fear the LORD your God as long as you live" (Deut. 6:2). Similarly, the book of Psalms is full of prayers for future generations. Legacy is a central message in the Bible.

David said it this way:

> Great is the LORD and most worthy of praise;
>   his greatness no one can fathom.
> One generation commends your works to another;
>   they tell of your mighty acts.
> They speak of the glorious splendor of your majesty—
>   and I will meditate on your wonderful works.
> They tell of the power of your awesome works—
>   and I will proclaim your great deeds.
> They celebrate your abundant goodness
>   and joyfully sing of your righteousness. (Ps. 145:3–7)

Our calling is to pray for our grandchildren. It's easy to feel overwhelmed; there are so many needs. Choosing to pray for one family each day of the week can make it easier to focus.

Also, we can create a list of the things we can pray regularly for our grandkids. Things such as:

They'd come to know Christ as their personal Savior at a young age.

They'd fall in love with the Word of God.

They'd recognize temptation and run from it.

They'd learn to make wise choices.

That if they are doing anything wrong, they'd get caught.

They'd learn to ask forgiveness from God and others and receive it.

That God would send strong role models their way.

They'd have close peers who love Jesus.

That God would be preparing mates for them who know and love Him first.

They'd be secure in their sexual identity as God has created them.

They'd remain sexually pure until marriage as God has commanded.

They'd develop close friendships with their parents and siblings.

They'd have a teachable spirit.

They wouldn't be devastated by failure but instead learn from it.

They'd have the ability to discern good from evil.

They'd have a sense of humor.

They'd learn to care for others.

They'd be people of integrity.

They'd learn to laugh at themselves.

This is not a complete list. You will add other items. And, over time, it's wonderful to watch how God answers. For example, we've seen our kids get caught doing something wrong in the most unexpected ways! It's good to get caught when you are young. We will talk more about our call to prayer in chapter 9.

The First Step in Planning a Camp: Prayer

Even before you begin to talk in detail about hosting a camp, pray. Pray with your spouse or other camp host and in your own private devotionals. You might write down the names of the kids coming and ask God to reveal to you what things to pray for them (reflect on chapter 2).

We have an abundant God who is delighted when we come to Him with our requests. One of my favorite Scriptures is Ephesians 3:20–21.

> Now to him who is able to do immeasurably more than all we ask or imagine, according to his power that is at work within us, to him be glory in the church and in Christ Jesus throughout all generations, for ever and ever! Amen.

Questions to Consider

1. What are some of your high hopes for planning a Cousin Camp?

_____

_____

_____

_____

2. Knowing yourself, where might you need to be ready to loosen (relax) your expectations?

_____

_____

3. What are some ways in which you can begin to pray for your grandchildren?

part 2

How to Host Your Cousin Camp

four

The Nuts and Bolts of Camp

This past summer John and I hosted our eleventh year of Cousin Camp. Just saying this seems incredible to me!

We began with five grandchildren from three different families. One family lived in Massachusetts, one in Virginia, and one in Pennsylvania. Because our kids were spread out, we wanted to provide a way for these cousins to get to know each other. And we wanted special time with them without their parents. Our long-term vision and prayer has been that *these kids would grow to love the Lord and love each other.* We knew that being with each other was necessary for their friendships to develop. And we also believed that, as grandparents, we could play a role in shaping their faith.

My friend Judy is a season ahead of us, and she had hosted a similar camp for her grandchildren. She became my tutor. One of her recommendations was to stipulate that campers had to be four years old to attend. This proved to be an important rule over the years. Four-year-olds are potty trained, sleep through the night (mostly), and have begun to learn to obey! And even when a parent lobbied for an "almost" four-year-old to attend, we held firm. It gave the younger ones something they could look forward to—a good life lesson.

Our camp is in June, when it's warm, and it lasts for four days and three nights. The parents drop the kids off and leave immediately, then return for a closing celebration on the last evening. Parents are not allowed at Cousin Camp! For the first seven years, John and I ran the camp by ourselves. But when we reached nineteen campers, we knew we needed help. It was a safety issue! So we asked a young couple from our church to come alongside us as "staff."

We hold camp at our small farm in the Shenandoah Mountains of Virginia. We set the dates in coordination with the parents one to two years ahead. With so many families our calendars get filled up quickly. Our target date is the first week after all the schools are out.

Many things go into planning camp. There are big items and small items. And each year there are changes.

Major Components

1. Preparation

Several months before camp, John and I have a planning meeting. The first thing we do is list the kids who will be coming that year and write down their needs. This enables us to assess current needs (as discussed in chapter 2) before we jump into designing our schedule. For example, Mac is four, so he will be a "newbie" this year. He might feel shy, and so we will enlist an older cousin to reach out to him.

After writing down needs and goals, we begin to sketch out the schedule for each day. We discuss what worked well last year and what we need to throw out this year.

We also discuss who's going to do what. It's easy for this to cause tension in our marriage, especially if we don't tackle it in plenty of time before the event. We have to work hard at communicating well, having realistic expectations, and covering for one another.

2. Good Communication

"It's here, it's here!" a child exclaims (usually a four-year-old!). What is it? The camp invitation. Each year, every child gets a hand-written invitation to camp. I could have something printed or emailed, but in today's world a handwritten "old timey" invitation seems novel and worth saving. Mine simply says: "You are invited to the Annual Cousin Camp," then includes the dates, location, and so forth. Some of the moms have saved all of these invitations.

A key component to planning is good communication with the families before camp. Along with coordinating the date for camp and inviting all the cousins, you'll want to get as much information from the parents as possible to help you plan. As camp gets closer, emails go out to the parents full of questions and requests.

Who should your child sleep near?

We've found sleeping siblings together when they are small makes them feel secure and less likely to stay up. Due to lack of space, our kids sleep in sleeping bags on floors, in closets, and on couches. The teens like sleeping in their own area and talking until the wee hours.

Are there special needs of which we should be aware?

Is your child anxious about anything? What is he or she most excited about? Are there allergies or meds of which we need to be aware? We have a high shelf where we put meds with specific instructions from the parents, and one of us is assigned to be the distributor. An older, responsible teen can also help with this.

What special gifts or interests does your child have?

We want to encourage these gifts, and we don't always know what they are, so this becomes our private "cheat sheet" that will help us plan our detailed schedule. (Remember, the schedule flows from needs and goals.) For example, one child is a natural "helper," another loves to cook, another likes crafts, and another likes to hammer anything!

As camp approaches, we exchange more emails with the parents. We want to know their arrival times, and we ask them to call five minutes out so those already here can rush out to welcome each new arrival. "Celebrating the greeting" is an important way to make folks feel welcome and wanted. We do this when the parents arrive at the end of camp as well, and often the kids hide in the bushes to jump out and race the cars up the drive.

Things are always evolving with camp. Many of the new ideas come from our kids. Each family has different favorite snacks. One daughter suggested each family bring (or ship) several bags of their favorite snacks. These snacks go into a special tub, which the kids get to choose from at specific times. Another option could be to have families bring snacks with their children, or for families to provide a list to the hosts in advance for purchase.

Each day we have an hour-long rest time. John and I need it! The kids do too, as it's easy to be overwhelmed by all the stimulation.

They don't have to sleep, but they do have to be alone. We make allowances for the older teens. Each family brings a rest time surprise for each of their children. From sticker books to coloring books to real books, this has been a huge help. It saves me hassle and money, and the parents know best what each child likes. The parents slip these to me when they arrive, and we give them out the first full day at rest time.

3. Buddies

Several months before camp, I usually get a call from a young grandchild asking, "Ghee, who is going to be my buddy this year at camp?"

The popularity of buddies has been one of the big surprises for us. John and I started a buddy system because we were desperate! When we hit eight grandchildren attending camp, we knew we needed help. We also wanted the older cousins to learn to reach out and to care for their younger cousins. At the beginning of camp, we give a simple explanation about the particular ways a big buddy might be helpful to a younger cousin. Then, throughout camp, we assign tasks and activities to buddies as appropriate. This is one practical way of training them to love each other. We post our list on the kitchen cabinets with all sorts of other information (flexible daily schedule, food for meals, Bible memory verse, and so on; see page 150 in the appendix, "A Photo of the Cabinets Covered with Everything"). Buddies help with filling water bottles, finding shoes and any lost items, writing in journals, doing crafts, filling plates at mealtimes, reading stories, and whatever else is needed.

As the years have gone by, some kids put in buddy requests. I make no promises, but I do keep their requests in mind. Everyone over age seven or eight has a younger buddy who is not a sibling. It has been amazing to me how this has bonded kids from different families.

Buddy Partners for Cousin Camp/ Family Camp

Note: all cousins ages 4 through 6 have big buddies.
Buddies last throughout both Cousin Camp and Family Camp.

Callie (17) for Grey (6); Callie and Grey together for Saylor (3) during Family Camp

Will (15) and Jack (8) for Fitz (4)

Tucker (13) and Blaine (7) for Mac (4)

Graham (10) for Alexander (5)

Tobin (11) for Hayes (5)

Cashel (9) and Davey (8) for Yates (4)

Sylvia (12) for Linden (6); Sylvia and Linden together for Sloan (3) during Family Camp

Isabel (10) for Mimi (4)

4. Goody Bags and Orientation Essentials

When all the children have arrived, it's time for the goody bags! We bring out plastic buckets or small totes labeled with their names, and the kids race to find theirs. Each contains some snacks, a small flashlight, an inexpensive water bottle with a self-attached top, and perhaps a small toy. We also write the child's name on every item with a permanent marker. Most items are from a discount store and will usually be lost by the end of camp. That's a realistic expectation.

Once the fun over the goodies has subsided, we have camp orientation, where we announce the buddies. We also post the buddy list. We explain camp rules: *Don't go to the pond, the barn, or the street by yourself. Don't eat food without permission.* (We have designated snack times, or the kids would be in my cupboards all day!) *No running or playing hide-and-seek in the house.* (It's an outdoor camp.) We try to have only essential rules.

Next, we take the new campers to a certain bathroom, pull out a step stool so small ones can reach the sink, turn on the water, and they fill their own water bottles. We tell them anytime they are thirsty, they can get their own water from this sink. Buddies will help them if needed. *Why?* This keeps them from asking us for water and keeps them from crowding the kitchen sink. Can you imagine five, ten, or even nineteen kids wanting us to get them water at the same time? The little ones are proud they can do it by themselves. They keep their bottles in a large tub when not in use.

One essential for camp is a digital clock for each sleeping area. We have a 7:00 a.m. rule. We tell campers they cannot leave their room in the morning until the clock shows 7:00. (We draw a sample for the little ones.) When a young one gets up too early, we send them back to their room. They soon learn we mean it.

A funny thing happened at the end of our first camp. During our closing ceremony with the parents, we asked each of the five kids to share what they liked about camp. I thought it might be the berry picking or a great craft or journaling or a certain game— those things I'd worked so hard on!

Tobin, age four, responded, "I liked the seven o'clock thing."

We laughed and explained what he meant to the parents, who were quick to take this new policy home!

5. Journals and Bible Study

The first year at camp each child receives a journal with his or her picture glued on the cover. We make a big deal presenting these. After breakfast we always have a Bible study time that John or I lead. The first thing we talk about is how we can each know

Jesus. We present a simple plan of salvation. (For a sample, see "The Plan of Salvation" in the appendix, page 140.) We ask each child if they would like to ask Christ into their life.

A simple prayer might be, "Jesus, thank You for dying on the cross for my sins. I ask You to come into my heart and live with me forever."

We don't pressure them. If they want to think about it, that's fine. Many have already done this. If a child seems ready, we let them choose who they might do this with and where they would like to do it. *Why?* It helps the big kids learn how to pray with a young child. And it makes it more of an event. The big kids always want to be chosen.

One year a grandson ignored his cousins' pleas to be chosen and said he wanted to do it with Poppy in the hammock. So off they went for a few minutes. We all clapped when they returned. Every child, often with the help of their big buddy, writes their own story in their journal about when and how they asked Jesus into their heart. Some have prayed this prayer at church, or with a parent, or in a car. Every year at camp, during the first Bible study, we go back and share these testimonies with each other. Most of the kids want to be the first to tell. It's positive peer pressure at work.

We know that children will have many times of recommitment in the future. They won't fully understand what they have done. They will have lots of questions. But they have taken this important first step. And God will grow each child in His time and in His way (Phil. 1:6).

For us this has been very natural. Young children are quite open and matter-of-fact. Grandparents can often make things more casual than parents.

We use the journals every day for writing down our camp theme verse or drawing a picture of a character in a Bible study we just heard. Buddies sit together, and big ones help little ones. In the back of each journal, we include a one-page explanation of "Assurance"

Four Things You Can Know for Sure

1. Jesus Loves You and Wants to Come into Your Life

Jesus knocks on the door of your heart. If you open the door and ask Him, He will come into your life, and He will never leave you.

Here I am! I stand at the door and knock. If anyone hears my voice and opens the door, I will come in. (Rev. 3:20)

Never will I leave you; never will I forsake you. (Heb. 13:5)

For God so loved the world that he gave his one and only Son, that whoever believes in him shall not perish but have eternal life. (John 3:16)

2. He Forgives Your Sins

When you ask Him to forgive your sins, He does!

If we confess our sins, he is faithful and just and will forgive us our sins and purify us from all unrighteousness. (1 John 1:9)

As far as the east is from the west, so far has he removed our transgressions from us. (Ps. 103:12)

3. You Can Know You Will One Day Go to Heaven

Going to heaven isn't dependent on being good enough to deserve it—no one is good enough to deserve heaven. It is a gift to those who have accepted that Christ died for their sins and given themselves to God.

Whoever believes in the Son of God accepts this testimony. . . . And this is the testimony: God has given us eternal life, and this life is in his Son. (1 John 5:10–11)

4. You Have the Holy Spirit to Help You Live the Christian Life

When Christ comes into your life, it is His Holy Spirit that comes in and gives you the power to live the life He has planned for you. He will give us the power to live. We can't do it on our own.

Since we live by the Spirit, let us keep in step with the Spirit. (Gal. 5:25)

You have a great, large family of other brothers and sisters in Christ who will help you grow up in Him.

(see "Assurance Letter" in the appendix, page 142). This explains what we can know with confidence once we accept Christ into our life. One year we gave each camper a five-by-seven laminated card entitled "Four Things You Can Know for Sure" (see appendix, page 144). It contained four simple things that will give us the assurance that Jesus will come into our hearts when we ask Him to and will never leave us, no matter what. We have found that too many adults and children lack this confidence. The campers took this home and stuck it in their Bibles. Their journals stay at our house during the year. This way they aren't lost and can be added to each year with the hope that one day they will be shown to the next generation.

6. Bible Study Ideas

You will need to adapt the Bible studies according to the ages of your campers. It is better to gear them to the middle or older kids rather than the youngest. Have a children's Bible handy. We recommend the *Jesus Storybook Bible* by Sally Lloyd-Jones. Also, you can ask parents to have their kids bring their own Bibles from home.

Below are three suggestions for you to use in your Bible study time with your grandchildren. We post the camp verse and tape it to the kitchen cabinet so they can memorize it. Each morning we say it together.

Don't worry if you feel your Bible study time flopped. It rarely goes as you'd like it to. But it will make a difference, and we have to remember God's Word does not return empty (Isa. 55:10–11). The Word of God is alive and active (Heb. 4:12). They are taking it in even if it is not evident at this moment!

7. Free Time and Rest Time

Kids get very little free time today. They are used to being entertained by someone or some device. Boredom has become unacceptable. This can encourage an unhealthy dependence on someone else—*It's your job to make me happy*—and it can stifle creativity.

Sample Bible Studies

EXAMPLE #1

Memory verse: "The whole earth is filled with awe at your wonders; where morning dawns, where evening fades, you call forth songs of joy." (Ps. 65:8)

Theme: Appreciating God's creation.

Application: Read Psalm 65. Have a child read or have several take turns—the more you involve the kids, the better. Before you read it, tell the kids you want each of them, as they listen, to pick out one phrase that they particularly like. You can have several tell theirs.

Questions for discussion:

1. What are three things you like about God's creation?
2. Can you think about where you experience your five senses (sight, sound, smell, taste, touch) in nature?
3. Draw a picture or write a song in your journal of something in nature for which you want to thank God. Take a few minutes to do this; buddies can help little ones. Then have volunteers show or read what they did.

You can carry this theme throughout your camp each day, using other nature passages and applications, or you can divide the above to use over several days.

Close in prayer, asking different children to pray or opening it up to all.

EXAMPLE #2

Memory verse: "The Lord himself goes before you and will be with you; he will never leave you nor forsake you." (Deut. 31:8)

Theme: Sometimes you will face difficult things, but you don't have to be afraid if you remember God is with you.

Application: Read Deuteronomy 31:1–8 (use kids for the reading as appropriate). You can assign roles and let the kids act out the story. It's fun to give them five minutes to run around and collect whatever they can find for a crazy costume. Ring a bell after five minutes. Act out the story.

Questions for discussion:
1. What is happening here, and how do you think these people are feeling, especially the Israelites, Moses, and Joshua?
2. What do verses 7 and 8 tell us about God? What is it about the promises that would have been encouraging to the Israelites, Joshua, and even Moses?
3. Can you think of something they have to do that is especially difficult for them?
4. Tell a story of how *you* have learned (or been reminded) that God was with you and how He helped you in a hard time. Have kids share their stories as appropriate.

Close in prayer, asking different kids to pray as appropriate.

EXAMPLE #3

Memory verse: "Let the peace of Christ rule in your hearts. . . . And be thankful." (Col. 3:15)

Theme: We can be thankful all the time no matter what is going on in our life at the moment. God is still in charge, and He will take care of us. It is easier to take Him for granted than to thank Him. Let's practice thanking Him.

Application: Have someone read the story of Jesus healing the ten lepers (Luke 17:11–19). This story is also fun to act out.

Questions for discussion:
1. What do you believe each of the different people were thinking? Why do you think they did what they did?
2. Let's see how many things we can think of for which we are thankful. Small children might draw a picture of something they are thankful for in their journal.
3. Think of a person you are thankful for and tell why. You can have some postcards for each child to write a note to that person, telling them they are thankful for them and why. Or they can write a note to that person and give it to them in person. Buddies help out. Give the completed postcards to the parents, and have them mail them.
4. Return to this theme of thankfulness each day in a variety of ways.

Close in prayer.

We bring back free time at camp. We have to explain what it is. "Now we are going to have free time. This is the time in which you can be creative. You can choose to play with someone else or choose to do something by yourself."

We have lots of options: bats and balls of every kind, wildflowers to pick, rocks to collect, puzzles, and crafts that don't need supervision. Devices are not permitted.

During our one-hour rest time each day, we also encourage creativity. We suggest the older kids write poetry or music; others draw a picture. Rest time is spent by yourself. The littlest ones often fall asleep. Rest time and free time can work well either inside or outside, depending on the ages of the children.

8. Camp Shirts

For our first several years, I went to a discount store and bought plain T-shirts and wrote "Cousin Camp" plus the year across the front of each one in permanent marker. My son-in-law, Scott, has an apparel printing company (www.threadbird.com), so he eventually took over designing and making our shirts. We wait to give out the shirts until right before the parents arrive for the closing ceremony. Otherwise they'd get lost. And that's when we take the official "camp photo." The kids wear their shirts for years.

9. Competitions

Two of our standard competitions are a ping pong tournament and a hula hoop tournament. The big kids make out the brackets for the contests. We've had some tears shed by kids who lose, but learning to lose is a part of life and they do recover! Each year we write the name of the ping pong winner on a paddle and nail it to the basement wall. We also hang a hula hoop on the wall with a hand-written wooden placard announcing the winner (see "A Photo of Our Champion Wall" in the appendix, page 145).

Other good games for camp include Jenga, Apples to Apples, board games, card games, and puzzles. These all work well on a rainy day!

10. Berry Picking and Cooking Class

Each year we drive to a local orchard and pick whatever happens to be in season: blueberries, raspberries, strawberries. Callie, our oldest grandchild, loves to cook, so she plans something to cook with the berries. It's usually popovers because they are easy. Buddies help the little ones make theirs. Also, everyone loves s'mores and expects this treat as part of our first night of camp.

11. Craft Time

Usually we have two sessions for making crafts. I always stock basic things: popsicle sticks, pipe cleaners, washable paints, tape, glue sticks, scissors, and markers. We have large, old painting T-shirts to wear over clothes for anything that might make a mess. Before camp, I go scavenging to houses under construction and ask the builders if they will save me a pile of small leftover wood. I collect this wood, and it has become the basis for one of our favorite projects. Be sure to stockpile several hammers and lots of nails with big heads. The kids go wild creating all sorts of buildings, planes, and nail puzzles.

When we started camp, I planned the crafts. Over the years, my daughter-in-law Alysia and her girls have taken over choosing, ordering, and preparing the crafts. They are much better at this than I am. Sylvia and Isabel have helped the younger cousins make tie-dye shirts and kerchiefs. Bead necklaces and bracelets are also always winners. There are numerous ideas for crafts available online.

A Sample Daily Schedule

Each year our schedule changes somewhat. We keep the things that worked last year and eliminate things that didn't! Usually the main

Sample Schedule

Sunday afternoon

Arrivals!

Snacks, goody bags, and camp orientation

Outdoor activities (hiking, swimming, horseback riding, playing in a creek, ball games, etc.)

Picnic supper and stories outside

S'mores and roasted marshmallows

Bedtime stories (You or older kids can read aloud. Funny voices can become new traditions.)

Lights out

Monday

Breakfast: after 7:00

Good morning prayer, journals, and Bible study

Outdoor activities

Free play

Lunch

Rest time (1 hour)

Snack time

Hike or other outdoor activity

Crafts

Free play

Supper

Bedtime stories

Lights out

Tuesday

Breakfast

Bible story with a craft, writing in journals

Horseback riding or another outdoor activity

Swimming

Free play

Lunch

Rest time (1 hour)

Snacks

"Camp closing" preparation: assemble goody bags for the arriving small children, tidy the house

The families arrive at 6:00 for supper and a "Closing Celebration" (details of this in chapter 6)

blocks in our daily schedule remain the same, but we change up some of the activities each year—remember, kids like consistency and variety. Our first year we had Cousin Camp for three days and two nights, then the rest of the families arrived and stayed for four more nights. In the following years Cousin Camp has been four days and three nights, with the parents arriving for four more days of Family Camp. (You can read about Family Camp in chapter 7.)

The previous page shows a typical schedule. We used this our first year with five kids: two girls, ages ten and five, and three boys, ages four, five, and eight.

Little Things That Can Make a Big Difference

Often, the little things we learn in the process can make a big difference. Here are a few:

We post the buddies, the meals, the camp memory verse, where everyone is sleeping, and the basic schedule (subject to change; we have a more detailed one we don't post). Posting these things helps to avoid tons of questions like "When will we . . . ?" "What will we . . . ?" The kids always race to see what's posted when they arrive (see page 150 in the appendix, "A Photo of the Cabinets Covered with Everything").

Shoe tubs! I got tired of tripping over shoes. Now we have forty-two different shoes! So we have shoe tubs by the back door—one for under-9s and one for over-9s. Shoes go in the tub as you enter the door.

Teams! Once our numbers grew, we began to divide our campers into two teams. We make up the teams ahead of time and try to split siblings up. We also designate team captains, and each team has a varsity and junior varsity component. This is merely to help us have smaller groups swimming in the pond at a time. But it also comes in handy for other activities. One year we had a blue team and a yellow team. Team members got a bandana in their color. This way they could recognize their teammates.

Delegate! Each year we turn more and more things over to the kids. *Why?* We want them to assume leadership, and often their ideas are better! For several years a couple of them made a playlist of favorite camp songs. For the past few years Callie has taken over the meal planning for camp. She recruits a cooking team to help at each meal. This has been a wonderful relief to me. She gives me a grocery list and I do all the shopping ahead.

Special talents! Isabel likes to sew. Several weeks before camp one year I asked her to sew a banner that we could hang. I gave her a few things I wanted to be included but then left it entirely up to her. When we presented the banner everyone cheered. It's one of my most precious things.

Since our camp is in June at our farm, we also have specific components related to country living: horseback riding, hiking, swimming in the pond, playing in the creek. You may not have access to "country things." It doesn't matter. Anywhere you live,

Design Your Own Banner!

- Draw your family tree
- Create a "coat of arms" with items important to your family
- Make up a family slogan or song
- Draw a picture of your family

you can find things to do. Cities have parks, and there are public pools, metros to ride, and museums to visit.

The events don't have to be a big deal. One of our favorites is to give each small child a small brown bag and go on a walk collecting only things that God has made (no cans or paper, etc!). When we come back from our walk, we take turns showing off our collection and telling what item we liked best. This simple activity helps us to *notice* what God has made in creation. Or we take the opposite approach and have the children pick up trash in a park or do another service project. Another time we collected rocks and painted them different colors.

Where you live is not that important. What will last are the little traditions you create and the bonding that takes place between your grandchildren.

Are you ready to make your plan?

You are about to have a blast. The next chapter is yours!

Questions to Consider

1. Which of the above components do you find most helpful?

_____

_____

_____

_____

2. When you dream about your own camp, what comes to mind?

_____

_____

_____

_____

3. What decisions do you need to make first, and what actions
do you need to take now as you consider a camp?

_____

_____

_____

_____

five

Designing Your Camp

I hope you are excited and ready to begin planning your event!

This chapter is going to be a bit unusual for the middle of a book. Most often a book dumps a lot of instructions on a reader. Then, at the end, you are supposed to implement everything you have read, but you barely remember it all. It can be overwhelming, and you hardly know where to begin.

This book is different. In the previous chapters you've read the basics about camp—the whys and hows, expectations and surprises. Now we'll pause the information and let *you* have the fun of beginning to create your own camp. But don't worry, we have more ideas to come. Spend some time here and start your own brainstorming. Take a deep breath, grab your spouse or a friend, and dream about *your* camp. You will find a lot of white space in this chapter. It is intended for your own planning. You may want to get some extra paper for additional notes. After reading the following chapters, you'll want to come back and add to your ideas.

It's YOUR Camp!

The purpose of this book is not to get you to copy our camp, it's to inspire you to create what is right for your family at this time in your lives. Everything about you is unique—your families of origin, your marriage, your kids, your grandkids. God knows us even better than we know ourselves. He knows what we need, and He will instruct us in how to go about planning what is best for our own family.

Think about the *fun* God the Father, Jesus His Son, and the Holy Spirit had in creating the earth. Oh, I wish I could have been there! Part of being created in His image is simply that He has also made us creative. He has given us imagination. And it thrills Him when we celebrate. A camp is a time to celebrate.

Grab some pens and paper and get creative!

A Few Things to Keep in Mind

As you begin to make your plan, start with prayer, asking for God to guide every step of your planning. You might also want to review the principles in chapter 2 on needs and goals.

Next, write a brief vision statement for your family—your prayer for your kids and grandkids.

Determine to start small, keep it simple, think outside the box, and in the process choose to love and to laugh.

Now, let's dig in! Consider the following questions:

1. Whom will we invite to our first camp, and what age do we want our campers to be? List your campers' names and ages. *One couple whose grandchildren all lived in the same town decided to have their Cousin Camp in two sessions, one for boys and one for girls.*

_____

_____

_____

_____

_____

2. When is the best time of year for our camp? *We do ours in the summer, but others have hosted at Thanksgiving, over Labor Day, or Christmas vacation.*

_____

_____

_____

_____

_____

3. How long should it last? *It is best to start small. You can always increase the length in the future. Consider the ages of the kids, the distance to travel to camp, and how they will get there.*

_____

_____

4. Where should we have camp?

Keep in mind you can have it anywhere, whether you live in a city or a rural area and have a small house or plenty of room. You simply adapt your activities to the place you are having your event. Brainstorm several possible locations.

5. How can we take advantage of our location?

Whether you live in a city or the country or the suburbs, research activities unique to your location that will appeal to the ages of your kids. Remember, it's the simple things that the kids will remember the most, like a meal in which everything has to be eaten with chopsticks—including Jell-O!

6. What will it cost?
   Identify your big expenses and determine how you will pay for them. You might begin a camp savings account and put a little in regularly throughout the year. Your kids may need to be financially responsible for getting their children to you.

   _____

   _____

   _____

   _____

7. Will we have a theme?
   One friend had "Christmas in July," and although camp was in the summer, everything they did was "Christmassy." We don't usually have a theme. We just call it Cousin Camp.

   _____

   _____

   _____

   _____

8. Now that we have an initial plan, who will do what next?
   For example, who will contact the kids about the dates and location? Who will send out the invitation to the campers? Make a list of assignments and the date by which each assignment is to be completed.

Beginning Your Checklist

As you read through the rest of the chapters, you will see things you want to remember. This chapter ends with more space for jotting those down and creating your checklist.

Now, before we move on, are you ready to have another brainstorming session?

What fun things would we like to do at *our* Camp?
Jot down everything you can think of, and remember this is to be a fun, creative brainstorming session. You can always go back and add to or delete from your list.

I hope you are excited. I'm excited for you. The next chapter will give you some ideas to add to your creative plans.

My Notes

Six

Developing Special Traditions

Traditions make camp feel personal and special. They bond your grandchildren more closely and become highlights of every camp. You will initiate some traditions at your first camp; others may simply evolve. Some special traditions are silly and fun, but others can be more solemn to mark the importance of the occasion and help children remember the moment.

Band of Cousins Ceremony

When we had our first camp, we began one of our core traditions: the BOC ceremony. "BOC" stands for Band of Cousins. This ceremony takes place on the last night of camp and it's just for the cousins. It's meant to promote a distinct legacy of camp. Every camper learns our special BOC pledge: *As cousins we pledge to serve the Lord and take care of each other always.*

The ceremony begins with a candlelight parade from the house to an outdoor shelter in our yard. The first year I used taper candles. They kept blowing out and dripping hot wax on small fingers.

Bad idea. We've switched to votive candles placed in small glasses. One camper is asked to be the leader and carry a large wooden cross made by the campers. Everyone processes in silence. At our first camp, John gave a brief message on God's two important commandments (Matt. 22:37–40). He explained how our pledge is meant to be one application of these commandments. The kids learn the pledge and each one recites it. This is their "initiation" into the Band of Cousins. We applaud each new camper, and John prays over them individually. At the end of our ceremony we have a little gift for every camper. The first year it was a hand-glazed pottery cross with a ribbon attached for hanging somewhere. I put their name and date on the back with a permanent marker. The kids don't jump up and down with joy (an unrealistic expectation). Whipped cream wars are much more fun! But this is something they can save that hopefully will bring back memories. I collect the BOC gifts at the end of the ceremony and put them on the mantle to save for their parents. Otherwise they'd get lost.

Since we have older teens at camp now, I asked two sisters to suggest an idea for the BOC gift this past year. They chose a leather bracelet (these are very "in" today!) that had the longitude/latitude of our farm stamped onto it along with a cross and the number 21 (representing the number of grandkids). It was a big hit, especially with the older kids. My husband still wears his. The BOC gifts aren't expensive, and they may not be used, but those who save them will have a sweet memory of a special summer.

This past year our campers ranged in age from seven to twenty-one. We knew we wanted the BOC ceremony to be a bit different. At every camp we have witnessed the powerful influence the older cousins can have on the younger ones. So, after our traditional candlelight parade and recitation of the BOC pledge, we had a special sharing time with ten of the big kids (who are ages eleven and over).

I prepped them in advance, explaining that I wanted each one to take about two minutes to answer three questions:

1. What Bible verse is one of your favorites, and why?
2. What is something you want God to do in your life in the coming year?
3. What piece of advice would you give to your younger cousins?

No one declined to participate—peer pressure, I expect! And it's hard to say no to a grandparent.

I did not know what they would say. But what they came up with was honest, vulnerable, encouraging, and left me and John in tears. Most powerful was the attentiveness of the younger cousins. Older role models who loved them were speaking truth into their hearts.

Why do we do this ceremony? Not only do we want our grandchildren to have crazy fun and build relationships but we also want them to understand, in a small way, the seriousness of commitment to one another. As the kids get older, we talk about what this might look like—those who one day will have financial resources sharing generously with those who don't; showing up when someone is in need. A couple of years ago one of our grandsons nearly died. He had to have a liver transplant. Each of his parents' siblings flew in to be with his parents. That's showing up.

More Big Traditions

In chapter 4, we covered the main blocks of camp. Here you will find a few more ideas about big traditions. You might want to circle the ones that apply to your situation and then go back to the previous chapter and add them to your developing plans.

Time Together in the Word

Each morning at camp we have a Bible study together. John usually picks the theme of the study, and most often it's a Bible character because people are easy to relate to. One year we chose Joseph. We emphasized the fact that God is working even when we can't see it. Another year John selected Samuel, and we talked about how God cares for and calls little children. It's important for each of us to listen for and to make time to hear His voice.

We choose a memory verse for each camp. The kids memorize it and write it in their journals. Buddies sit together, and the big kids help the little ones write or draw. Morning Bible study doesn't last more than about thirty-five minutes. As the kids mature, we ask them to help lead the study. Their leadership is more powerful to the younger ones than mine or John's.

When our own children were small, we learned a "good morning" prayer that we prayed at the breakfast table. At camp we begin our Bible study with this prayer, and John and I both find ourselves often praying it in our own quiet times throughout the year. It goes like this: *"Good morning, dear Lord. This is Your day. I am Your child. Please show me Your way."*

Our little grandson Tobin decided we needed one to say at bedtime, so he wrote this: *"Good night, dear Jesus, the day has now ended. When the morning bird calls let us wake up again."*

Seeing the creativity in our grandkids is one of the sweet joys of camp.

The Big Adventure

Every camp needs one big adventure. Two of our most popular have been scavenger hunts and obstacle courses. We divide the campers into two teams. If you choose to use teams, you can keep them the same throughout camp or occasionally mix them up to help the children get to know each other and divide skills appropriately. If possible, it's good to separate siblings.

We create the scavenger hunt list before camp. It might include things to find: a dogwood leaf, bark from a sycamore tree, a worm, or a song to compose and sing. The older the kids get, the more difficult the items become. Because we want the kids to use up some energy, the hunt involves running all over the property. A local park would work just as well.

Once we got some "staff" (a young couple from our youth ministry), the obstacle course became a highlight. They planned ahead, bought needed supplies, and early in the day laid out the course. We quietly asked two of our oldest campers to help with the setup. This event was such fun that we left it up for "Family Camp" and had all the dads do it in one team and then the moms. Their kids cheered wildly. And the moms won! (You can watch some of our camp videos on my blog, susanalexanderyates.com. Search Cousin Camps.)

Manners Training

One of the ways we can support our own children is by teaching and reinforcing their kids' good manners. Every year we have a "good manners—bad manners" skit. A couple of the older kids act out a bad way to greet someone (hang your head, mumble, don't speak or look them in the eye) and then a good way (look them in the eye, say "Hello, I'm . . . ," offer your hand to shake theirs). We make it very funny. Every camper has to practice greeting someone properly before we move on to a fun activity.

Why do we do this? Good manners are a means of showing respect, and respect is an important character trait.

Conversation Training

We also have "conversation training" for the older kids after the little ones go to bed. We realized that in today's culture, kids often don't know how to engage another person in simple conversation. We divide into two teams, and these teams come up

85

with good questions to ask a younger child, a peer, and an adult. The questions must call for more than a one-word answer and are even better if they have a follow-up question. For example, to a younger child: "What's your favorite sport?" "What do you like to do at recess?" To a peer: "Who is someone you admire? Why?" "What has been your favorite family vacation? What made it so good?" To an adult: "What is a typical day like for you at work?" "Who is someone who has made a positive impact on your life?" "How?" "What book have you enjoyed this year?"

The kids get very creative and also a bit competitive in developing thoughtful ways to have a conversation. We've also found it helpful to come up with two categories for developing good conversations: schedules and relationships. Everyone has schedules and relationships. "What's your class schedule like?" "Who are some of your best friends?" You can make a list of questions that fall into one of these categories.

Why do we do this? Most kids and adults do not know how to engage with someone else. It's awkward. Yet it is a practical way of learning to care for another person. We want our grandkids to have good manners and to be mindful and caring of others. And these exercises help us adults to become better conversationalists as well. (For more ideas, see page 145 in the appendix, "'Raising Good Conversationalists' Blog Post.")

Affirmations

We've added new things to camp as ideas percolate. Two years ago, we added an "Affirmation Box." Each day (or throughout the day), kids can write a brief affirmation about someone else and slip it into the box. We look through them and add as needed so every child receives some. We may enlist an older camper to write one for a young child. Each evening we read some from the box.

Here are samples of the affirmations:

To Cashel
   I notis that you chekt on mac. I like that. Love Mimi

To Davey
   I really liked the way you held the box for everybody.
It was very nice. Love, Yates

To Sloan
   You are like a 2nd sister to me. Love, Grey

And I even got one; it's precious to me!

Ghee,
   You alwase make me happy at night and evry other
okashion.

Our purpose is to teach the kids to notice the good in others and to appreciate them. We hope this will carry over when they go home!

Recently our daughter Libby sent me a picture of an affirmation that her eight-year-old son Fitz wrote to his brother Yates. (This was his idea. His mother did not prompt him.) Their family had been talking about one of their family values: encouragement.

Yates I really like you. you are a really good brother You are
so good at socker. You are a good atlileat. You should grow up
to be a coach. You are amazing! Love, Fitz.

Maybe they did learn something at camp!

The Closing Celebration

Your grandkids have invested time and energy and made many memories. One way to celebrate their time together is a closing celebration. This is one of the highlights of our camp. The closing celebration occurs on the evening parents and younger grandchildren arrive for Family Camp. The campers plan this celebration with our help. We do our planning in the afternoon right before the parents come, and it takes about two hours. They make goody bags for the little brothers and sisters who are coming.

Parent Competitions

One of the most fun things is designing a competition for the dads. One year we came up with "How well do you know your child?" We blindfolded the dads and put a shower cap (from hotel giveaways) over each child's hair. The children then lined up, and each dad had to feel the face of every child and guess which one was his.

We have also done scavenger hunts for the parents. The kids create a list and send their parents (divided into teams) on a hunt.

Here's one of our funniest prizes for the dads: we blindfolded the dads to give them their "prizes," which were disposable diapers filled with melted chocolate. The kids joyfully smashed these "prizes" into their dads' faces.

Nicknames

Every child chooses a nickname. You can do this at the beginning of camp and use the names all week, or choose them on the last day before the closing celebration. We choose them on the last day because we can't remember them all throughout the camp with so many kids! We read them out and the parents have to guess who each one is. Our grandkids have chosen names like "Rocking Rodeo Rider," "Mr. Scoop," "Boots Boy," and "Cheek Girl." This activity is funny, easy, and can be done with any age.

Dress Up Clothes

Thrift stores and yard sales are a good resource for filling a dress up box with fun clothes. We assign a Bible story to two teams of cousins and give them a half hour to act it out, dressing up in anything from the box or anything else they can find. It's hysterical. And it's really hilarious to get the parents to do this as well.

An Amazing Dessert

For our first camp, I bought a long piece of roof gutter at the hardware store. We line the gutter with aluminum foil and fill it with lots of ice cream, bananas, and other toppings, and it becomes "Warren County's Largest Banana Split." The first year the kids had to eat it without hands or spoons. They decided that was gross, so in subsequent years we've allowed spoons, but someone, usually a parent, still ends up with whipped cream all over their face!

There are many reasons we end Cousin Camp with a special all-family celebration or meal.

1. It gives the parents a picture of what camp has been like.
2. Parents are able to see their kids in the context of being with their cousins.
3. Parents learn things about their children that they may not have been aware of before.
4. It puts a happy exclamation point on a family gathering.
5. It evokes healthy laughter, and laughter is good for every family.

> "Our mouths were filled with laughter, our tongues with songs of joy. . . . The LORD has done great things for us, and we are filled with joy." (Ps. 126:2–3)

Questions to Consider

1. What are three to five traditions that you would like to have at your camp?

2. Describe two of the above in detail.

3. What actions do you need to take for these to be established (i.e., what materials are needed, who will get them, and when)?

part 3

Beyond
Cousin Camp

*Creating Different Types
of Family Gatherings*

seven

Family Camp and Extended Family Reunions

Larger family reunions that include the adults can be a wonderful time for your children to get to know your siblings' spouses and their nieces and nephews. They are particularly helpful for families who don't live near one another and are rarely able to be together. It gives our children a sense of something much bigger than their own unit. A sense of belonging is important to each one of us.

Each summer at the end of our four-day Cousin Camp we begin our Family Camp, which lasts for three more nights. We plan these camps back-to-back because this works best for us logistically with families living in different states.

Remember, your family is unique. Don't try to copy us or anyone else. You may want to start small with a twenty-four-hour or one-day Cousin Camp and a family evening after Cousin Camp. This book merely gives ideas and examples. Ask God to show you what is best for you—and this may change from year to year.

Getting on the Same Page

Before Family Camp, one of my adult children creates and sends out an email questionnaire to all the adults. The answers are then shared with the other adults. This enables us to catch one another up on current news and learn fun facts so that we don't have to repeat things over and over when we first arrive.

We have a few who don't love this assignment, but we insist they complete the questionnaire before dropping their children off at Cousin Camp—or they'll be turned away! Sometimes there's a bit of competition to see who can send theirs in last.

Some of the questions have been:

What is something new you have learned about yourself this year?

What are your favorite reads, listens, and/or viewings from the year?

What is a skill you'd like to learn in the coming year and why?

What is something you've enjoyed learning about/watching in each of your children in this year (a proud moment, area of growth, or anything else)?

What has been a prominent focus (theme/challenge/joy) for you this year?

Since we were last together, what is the most fun thing you have done?

What is the hardest thing you have accomplished?

When were you happiest and when were you saddest?

What is the hardest thing you've had to deal with?

What is the best thing you've learned these past twelve months?

What is your best purchase of the year? Why?

What have you been reading?

What is the best advice you received or gave this year?

What is something unexpected from your year—something
you were grateful for and/or something that was hard?

What is one habit you'd like to cultivate this year in yourself?

What is one habit you'd like to cultivate in your children?

What is your proudest/happiest/best parenting moment this
year?

Name the child who is most like you and how/why.

What is your favorite thing about where you are living?

What is one thing you look forward to in the next year?

These questions have enabled us to get to know one another in
ways that we might not make time for in the day-in and day-out
stresses of life, and they allow us to come together already feeling
a little caught up with one another.

Family Camp Begins

Excitement builds. The cousin campers start picking up their
clothes, straightening their rooms, and, with their buddies' help,
tidying assigned areas: bathrooms, yard clutter, and so forth. It's
a straightening, *not* a deep clean! Giggles abound as the kids talk
about what they have planned for their parents.

Just before the parents arrive, the race begins to hide from them.
The parents call when they are five minutes away. Kids crouch
behind bushes or climb on rocks, eager to scream and cheer, jumping from hiding places when a car pulls in and racing the car up
the drive.

It's the official beginning of "Family Camp."

What Does Family Camp Look Like?

In the early years, the parents arrived with children under age four
who did not yet qualify for Cousin Camp. We wanted these little

ones to feel welcomed too, so once all arrived, the campers brought out goody bags for the younger cousins. These varied from plastic buckets to sacks filled with small flashlights, crayons, a snack, a small toy, and so on. We assigned each older camper to be a buddy to someone under four. Their job was to help the parents and assist the little ones in everything!

It's a good idea to start family gatherings with a kickoff event. Our first official event is supper all together: a picnic outside. Supper is followed with the "Warren County's Largest Banana Split" we mentioned in the previous chapter. Yours might be lunch and an outdoor activity or family game. The key is involving everyone and setting the tone for the event.

Because our dinner is both the start of Family Camp and also the closing of Cousin Camp, after dinner we present a "Closing Celebration" for Cousin Camp that the cousins have created with our help (see chapter 6 for details). This is always a highlight.

At the Closing Celebration, we give out camp shirts to the cousins. Some years, the adults get them too. The colors and designs vary. We ask a neighbor to come take the "official family photos." We know if we wait, shirts will get lost! And gathering everyone for pictures can be a nightmare, so we do it right away while excitement is high and cooperation is more likely.

A Giant Slumber Party

Now that our family consists of thirty-three people when we are all together, finding spots for everyone to sleep can be challenging. In this respect, Family Camp looks like a giant slumber party (hosted by grandparents who just might be losing their minds!). Before Family Camp I get suggestions from our adult kids about what would be the best sleeping arrangement for their kids. Those with youngest children are given priority, and usually families sleep together, using floors, closets, and sleeping bags. Generous neighbors share extra rooms in their homes for overflow. We've also pitched a tent, which the older teens enjoy. We have all learned to lower expectations for lots of sleep. Reunions are not about rest; they are about connecting. Don't forget to include your sleeping arrangements in your chapter 5 checklist!

The year Libby and McLean brought their two-year-old quadruplets for the first time, we put them in one room. Within a few minutes they had thrown every book off its shelf onto the floor, pulled mattresses onto the floor, and basically "trashed" the room. When I peeked in, I burst out laughing. Libby cried. We firmly put them back in their beds and sent an older cousin in to monitor them until they fell asleep. The next night I took one of them to a neighbor's house to sleep there with me.

With eight grandchildren age six and under (plus thirteen others) this was by far our most exhausting year.

Was it worth it? Definitely!

Why?

Libby and McLean's siblings got to experience firsthand what their life is like—with five children in two years. We also assigned two older cousins to each quad and a team to help Libby and McLean each day, so they could enjoy a bit of a rest as well.

We got to connect with one another even in the chaos. There is something special about sharing real life, the difficult times as well as the fun times. We have hysterical stories to tell—eight years later, they are funny, though not so much at the time! We continued a tradition that has provided so many memories and enabled cousins to build relationships.

More Laidback than Cousin Camp

Whether you start big or small, keep the mood relaxed. Our Family Camp is a little less structured than Cousin Camp. I still post a schedule because the grandkids want to know what is happening next. We usually have a morning Bible study (thirty minutes max) led by John and some campers, then free time until lunch.

We post a list of free time activities. After lunch there is rest time, and then a couple of the parents host some events that they can plan ahead, such as a soccer, corn hole, or badminton tournament, or perhaps a carpentry activity. And there is always hula hooping! Ask your children what their kids' favorite games are. Have some of these on hand, or ask each family to bring their favorite one for the group.

When we move from Cousin Camp to Family Camp, a transition occurs. Family Camp is not just for the kids; it's a time for the adults to engage with each other. For the kids, this takes some adjustment from the planned activities of Cousin Camp.

"Mama, will you . . . ?" a child will ask. Sometimes a parent will respond, "Not now, I'm talking to your aunt. This is your time to go and play a game with your cousins."

Over the years, we have developed a long list of activities. This list is posted year-round in the hall. The top of our list says, "We don't say I'm bored or there's nothing to do." None of the activities listed requires an adult. Over the years the kids have added to the list. (See "'Things to Do' List" on page 151 in the appendix to see how our list has grown over the years.)

Gather the kids together and make it a challenge to see how many unusual activities they can come up with for your location. Post the list.

Meals

We ask each of our adult couples to be in charge of food for one day, keeping in mind the circumstances of each family. Two couples can share a day if needed. They plan, purchase, cook, and clean (with their kids' help) on their assigned day. This enables everyone else to have time off without feeling guilty. Most meals are buffet style, served on paper plates, and eaten outside. Lunch is usually salads and sandwiches. Except for the first night's arrival ceremony, we feed the children dinner early and then the adults eat once the smallest are put to bed. The older cousins are in charge of babysitting, and we let them watch a family-friendly movie or play games. We also set aside time for smaller gatherings.

Gals Lunch Day

One lunch, usually on our first full day, we six girls (my five daughters and I) go out to lunch and leave the men in charge of the kids, including feeding them and cleaning up. We are usually gone two hours. This gives us a break and enables us to finish a sentence!

Activities List

Sleep	Hula hoop
Read	Paint rocks
Climb trees	Build a fort
Play ping pong	Play Frisbee, soccer,
Play with trains	baseball, or football
Color	Write a song or a
Play freeze tag	poem
Work a puzzle	Create a scavenger
Play dress up	hunt or a play
Write in journals	Play with LEGOs
Write on basement	String beads
floor (or driveway)	Play hide-and-seek
with chalk	Look at photo albums
Cook	or old family movies
Play with blocks	Play tea party
Get a cup and collect	
worms and bugs	

Guys Lunch Day

The next day the women take over and the guys go out. Male bonding takes place during a big meal and often a trip to the local country hardware store. You can adapt these ideas to fit your time together. For instance, for a one-day gathering, the guys might go out for breakfast and the gals go out for lunch.

Adult Meals

For Family Camp, we have adult-only dinners after the kids have eaten. Our adult children decide who is cooking what, and the cook of the day prepares a nice meal. Most of my children like to cook or married cooks. They didn't get that from me! We eat in a shelter about fifty yards from the house, mainly for the quiet. The kids are told not to interrupt us unless it's an emergency. These adult meals include a time of sharing. Each couple shares the blessings and challenges of their past year and the things for which they need prayer. When they finish we pray over that couple. This enables us to go deeper in our relationships. It's a very precious time that has become more natural over the years.

For your gathering, you can have different adult and children's meals as appropriate for the ages of your family.

Extended Family Reunions

John and I each have three siblings. All of our siblings have several children. Together we have twenty nieces and nephews, spread out across the country. It's not practical for us to get together on a regular basis. But we do want to stay connected, so every several years we gather. Each reunion is different. It's important to consider who is coming and plan an event that will be an encouragement to that particular set of people. Therefore, in planning each event we review the needs and goals discussed in chapter 2. Here are three different examples.

A Big Extended Family Reunion

Several years ago, we hosted my siblings and their kids and grandchildren at our farm. We used hotels nearby for overflow. It began on the Thursday of Labor Day weekend and closed with a brunch on Labor Day. This weekend was in honor of our parents, Mimi and Doc, who were already in heaven. Included were their four children, grandchildren, and great-grandchildren. My folks would have loved it!

Several things will help make a big reunion work.

1. Set the date early and delegate responsibilities.

The larger your reunion, the more important it will be to get an early date on the calendar, particularly if families are coming from afar. We set the date a year out for our big reunion to get it on everyone's schedules. Once my siblings agreed with the idea and date, I began to plan in more detail. I have learned that it's important to have the next generation "buy in" to any reunion plans. A niece or nephew is more likely to respond to an aunt than a parent, so I enlisted one niece from each of the families to make up my planning committee! I set up a conference call to brainstorm ideas. An initial conference call is better than emails, because enthusiasm is generated and ideas are stimulated when we're talking. And it's fun to connect people who have not been in touch.

It is important to involve a lot of the next generation in creating a plan for your reunion. For our reunion, the adult cousins came up with some great ideas. Sarah volunteered to design and order cousin T-shirts. Caroline and Susy produced a pre-reunion "Alexander Anecdotes" (see appendix, page 152). They emailed questions to everyone and created an informative newsletter from their answers. It was similar to what we do with our Family Camp adult update emails but even more extensive. Many of the next generation attending were meeting each other or spouses for the first time. Being a little up-to-date on each person before arriving made the initial gathering less awkward and set the tone for a great weekend.

Frances suggested that we have a project anyone could work on. Projects enable folks to get to know one another in a natural way. So we asked some of the dads to design a treehouse. We bought the lumber ahead of time and constructed it over the weekend. It was a brilliant idea. My brother Frank is interested in genealogy, so he prepared a talk for all of us about our heritage, a competitive quiz on our ancestors, and some hysterical stories on "old people" from long ago. Included was an amazing family tree.

As you plan your family reunion, consider the gifts and personalities of your extended family and play to their strengths. People like to contribute their own gifts. This will make them feel more invested in the success of the reunion.

2. Use a community facility or conference center.

Sometimes family members' homes will not be large enough to accommodate a big reunion. Determine your location based on your own needs.

For example, several years ago John's sister organized a "Tucker Reunion" that included lots of first, second, and third cousins all somehow related to "Granny Tucker." Because there were about a hundred people, we met over Memorial Day weekend at a church conference center in the mountains of North Carolina. One additional advantage of meeting there was that the conference center provided the food! We had name tags for everyone, a snack room to which all contributed, and crafts organized by one of the moms. A couple of dads created relay races, and there was a pool for swimming. Our time was more "hang out" rather than scripted, which worked well with so many people who wanted to visit with one another.

One five-year-old girl told her mom she liked how safe she felt exploring the property on her own with a cousin because everywhere she went there was someone she was related to!

3. Pick a central location and consider catering.

On another occasion, cousins hosted a one-day retreat in a central location. One meal was catered, and an organized time of sharing was planned. Babies cried and toddlers ran around, but it was successful because the expectation was simply to connect with relatives we had not seen in a while.

Special Gatherings

John is the youngest of four children, so we have the youngest kids. With such big families it's hard to have time alone with adult siblings. A few years ago, we hosted an adult—OK, "old folks"—reunion with his three siblings, their spouses, and a close first cousin and his wife. We were all in our mid-sixties to early eighties. The contrast between this group and Cousin Camp couldn't be greater. We all *liked* to go to bed early. We *liked* quiet. We *liked* to linger over meals. We *didn't* expect or even want to be entertained every minute. We *liked* down time. We *didn't* care about devices. We *liked* to eat more than hot dogs or mac 'n' cheese!

We all agreed that we also liked getting older. This doesn't mean we liked the aches and pains. But all in all, we have learned what really matters in life, and we don't feel quite so pressed to prove ourselves as we did when we were younger.

Since we had more years under our belts and because we thought a theme for our time together would be good, we made a plan. Throughout our time we took turns looking back in segments of twenty years. We asked the question, "Where did you see God's faithfulness in the first twenty years of your life?" Later we shared about the second twenty years, then the third twenty years. Our goal was twofold: to focus on God's faithfulness and to get to know each other in new ways. We learned surprising things about one another that we did not know! Our cousin's wife shared that she had been born blind. While her family wasn't particularly one of faith, she did have a godly grandfather. This grandfather went to see every pastor in her small town and asked them to put her on their church's prayer list. She completely recovered her sight! There were many other sweet stories of God's blessings, and we realized afresh that one of the joys in getting older (not old, mind you!) is that it meant we had lived long enough to have a larger collection of stories of God's faithfulness and to have seen the truths of Romans 8:28 come to fruition. Focused conversations keep us from complaining and instead encourage thanksgiving.

Small Get-Togethers

Because John and I have so many grandchildren, and therefore they have so many first cousins, we decided to make a special effort to do some smaller events. We created what we call a "Double Digit Trip." When a grandchild is in the double-digit years, usually between the ages of eleven and fifteen, we take three grandkids from three different families who are close in age away for a few days. Our purpose is to connect cousins with one another in a smaller setting, and also for us to get to interact with a smaller group of our grandkids.

Our trips haven't been fancy. We drive to keep costs to a minimum. We do stay in a hotel with a swimming pool and get two rooms. John and I want to sleep! Our first trip was a "roots trip"— to North Carolina to visit the homes in which we grew up, a funky pottery town, and the legendary Smith Center in Chapel Hill. We took a different group to Pittsburgh to see a Pirates baseball game and visit the birthplace of one of the grands. With the third group we visited Amish country in Pennsylvania and Hershey Park. One of the grands always makes a small photo book with funny one-liners for each of us at the end of the trip. Our goal is to build memories and relationships.

Your Family Is Unique

Whatever event you might plan, remember that no two families are alike. We are each different, with unique needs and other factors to consider.

The purpose of a reunion is to connect. It's not a time to highlight political, theological, or social differences. It's not wise to use these few days to discuss sticky subjects, to argue for your perspective, or to jump on your own soapbox. This would be a distraction and sow seeds of discord. Use other times throughout the year to engage in tough topics. At this time choose to focus on the other person, asking questions that demonstrate you are interested in them. Questions like, How has your year been? What is a typical day like in your job? Have you read any good books lately? What are you looking forward to in the coming year? Who is someone you admire?

My friend Sally comes from a very dysfunctional family. Many of her family are not believers; in fact, some are antagonistic to faith. Several have struggled with addictions. However, Sally felt that hosting a camp would bring a measure of healing to a hurting family. She learned to adjust her expectations and not compare her family to someone else's.

She planned a reunion that would have a broad appeal. It was a big hit and a small step in building relationships. Of course, things did not go as planned. They never do, no matter what the family is like. She said, "You have to accept your reunion for what went well and let go of the rest."

The banner over any reunion should read "Grace Reigns Here."

In planning your event, don't copy us or anyone else, but glean ideas from others that might be adjusted to work in your situation.

With God's help, you will be able to create something very special that years from now, when some cousins are sitting around together watching *their* grandkids play, they might just say, "Remember that time we . . . !"

Questions to Consider

1. What have you read in this chapter that you want to consider for your family? Go back and circle ideas that you liked, or write them in here.

2. What other types of reunions would you like to consider for your family, and when would it be most appropriate to have one?

3. What family members might you involve in your planning?

eight

What Others Have Done

Every family has unique needs, so each Cousin Camp or Family Reunion will be different. The goal is to think through the needs of your family and plan what will work best for you. Don't be afraid to make changes for future events. (See chapter 2 to review planning principles.)

Here are some ideas from others who have hosted a camp. You might circle the ideas you like, flip back to chapter 5, and insert them into your own plans.

Willa and John

Willa and John have hosted three cousin camps. They began with four children ages six and under from two different families. This year they allowed a three-year-old sister to join in. There is one boy in this gang of five cousins. They've hosted camp in two different places, once at the beach in the summer and the next year in the fall at their home. Their camp is on a weekend, from Friday to Sunday afternoon.

Each year they choose a Bible verse and a theme related to the verse. "You are the light of the world. A town built on a hill cannot be hidden" (Matt. 5:14) was the verse one year, so they planned activities and discussions centered around light and dark.

Willa purchased several glowsticks and neon necklaces, and the kids got to stay up late. Once it was dark, they all went outside, where they recited their Bible verse over and over, each time getting another glowstick until the backyard was filled with light. Throughout camp, Willa, John, and the kids discussed what it meant to be the light of the world.

The year they held camp at the beach, their theme was "In all these things we are more than conquerors through him who loved us" (Rom. 8:37). They built sandcastles on the beach and talked about how the castle had to have a firm foundation in order not to fall.

"In order to be conquerors, we need a strong foundation," they told the kids. "Our foundation is Jesus."

Watching one sandcastle that had not been built on a strong base fall over was a great visual!

Willa and John also use a lot of music. They download songs that are easy to sing throughout camp. Their kids sing a lot. They found a YouTube video of a song about being conquerors that had hand motions. The kids loved this. A blessing of the internet is that you don't have to be musical to have singing at camp!

"Willa," I asked, "what is something you did at camp that did not work?"

"The first year we let them all sleep in the same room! They were too young and didn't sleep, which made for grumpy grandparents and whiny kids the next day. The next year we separated everyone at bedtime!"

"What are a couple of things that surprised you?"

"Our one grandson got bored with some of the crafts because they felt too 'girly.' So we set aside 'one on one' time for him with his grandad while the girls did something else. This small adjustment made a big difference.

"We also factor in free time every day. It's important for the kids to have down time and to be creative. During one free time I discovered my six-year-old granddaughter and my three-year-old granddaughter sitting at a table with the chess board out and players somewhat arranged.

"'Does Ruth (age three) know how to play chess?' I asked the six-year-old.

"'No, but I'm teaching her!' she said. She did not know how either, but what was precious was that they were making something up during free play! That's creativity at work.

"What the kids love the most," observed Willa, "is being silly together and having time without their parents, as well as the mix of active times, quiet times, and times to learn about Jesus."

Catherine

Catherine, who is single, is a favorite aunt. Single people play an important part in building strong families too! Catherine has chosen to invest in her nieces and nephews. She lives in a country home in England, and she has a passion to steward the land. She's also a busy lawyer. Her love for her family and for animals is a strong component in her DNA.

Several years ago, Catherine began to host a Farm Camp for her nieces and nephews and some neighborhood children. Being single enables her to have some flexibility in her schedule. She first visited farms to learn about land conservation and the care and nurture of farm animals, then started her project in a small way by acquiring some sheep and several goats. The goats didn't last long, as they kept running away! She then added chickens and a pony.

Catherine has taught the children how to clean out stalls, mix food, and move slowly around animals. Two of her lambs were rejected by their mother, so they spent time being fed and cared for in a large dog pen in her kitchen. Cleaning up their messes was a lesson in real life! The children have learned how to be gentle and calm. And they've had lessons in responsibility and hard work.

I asked Catherine's mother, Suzy, what she had observed from watching her daughter care for the children.

"Catherine has brought our whole family together. She's instilled in each one of us a sensitivity to God's creation. It's so easy for me, being a city person, to focus on buildings, pavement, shops—really man's creation—and to neglect to focus on God's creation, which is best exemplified in nature. Catherine could be focusing on herself and travel and fun opportunities, but instead she has chosen to invest in the lives of her nieces, nephews, and neighbors' kids. Her unselfishness and intentionality are a huge encouragement to me."

Frank and Joan

Frank and Joan recently held their first camp. They decided it was best to host their four grandaughters first and plan a camp for the boys the following summer. Since the children were young, they limited their first camp to twenty-four hours. All of the grandchildren live in the same city, so travel wasn't an issue. They picked up the kids and drove to their rural country house. Having time in the car listening to the girls interact was a good way for them to start.

Their purpose was to begin to help these cousins bond. Even when families live in the same city, it can still be difficult to get together. And Frank and Joan wanted their grandchildren all to themselves.

Because Joan is an elementary school teacher, she's adept at making lesson plans and collecting materials. She ordered everything online and planned the crafts in advance. She thought she'd have more than enough planned, but she learned that little kids with short attention spans go through things much faster than older ones, so it helps to bring too much! Two favorite crafts were making butterflies out of coffee filters and making tissue paper turtles.

One of the big hits was the "sundae party," with lots of ice cream and toppings to choose from. Especially sprinkles. When Grandma wasn't watching, one child poured half a jar of sprinkles onto her ice cream, making a gray soup. Of course, the others did the same. It was hysterically gross.

The kids kayaked in the pond (wearing life jackets, of course) and learned how to jump out of the boat. It was a "first" for them, and scary, but they were proud of themselves. A "field trip" across the street to a farm family inspired these city kids as they learned about vegetable gardening and played with pigs and goats!

Some special activities included a bubble bath for the girls, eating M&M pancakes for breakfast, and curling up and reading books at bedtime. They also did mani-pedis with lots of different colors, and even got their papa in on it! Now at family gatherings they all want to paint Papa's toes!

Frank and Joan describe their first camp this way: "There was something special about being able to focus on the girls and also to be able to watch them interact with one another. It was fascinating to watch three girls close in age playing together. We were surprised to see who was the dominant one. Leadership changed with each activity. What fun to see their personalities begin to blossom. This gave us hints in how to build their strengths in the future. Starting with four girls for twenty-four hours was just right for our family."

Kim and Penelope

Kim and Penelope, who live in a small village in the UK, host six grandchildren from three different families. Their grandkids' camp lasts two nights and three days and is held in their home.

They choose a theme for their camps. One of their favorites has been "Crazy Cousin Camp." During this camp they tried to make everything crazy—having Christmas in July, walking backward, going to bed fully dressed, sleeping at the foot end of the bed, eating Jell-O with chopsticks, making Christmas decorations.

Another hit was "Wild Cousin Camp." One night they had a "Moonlight Meander" with a "Marshmallow Munch." They kept the kids up late and took them outside to watch the stars and look for bats. Hot chocolate, marshmallows, and staying up way past bedtime made this a really fun night! Their campers watched a film of Bear Grylls in the woods and read his adventure stories each night. The boys loved this. They all loved picking berries from the countryside hedges, making paint with them (a mix of salt, water, and squashed berries), and tie-dying T-shirts.

Penelope chooses their camp themes from free resources available online. LEGO once did a promotion that included free exercise charts, stopwatches, and posters for kids. With small kids, her "LEGO Camp" was a big hit. She also ties in Bible stories each morning to fit the theme.

Mary

Mary's mother has hosted many family reunions for her grandchildren. A favorite memory that marks each gathering has been the "Biggest Birthday Celebration Ever"! They set aside one day to celebrate all the birthdays of the past year. There is always a theme: Hawaii, pirates, clowns, superheroes, and so on. Usually there's a big treasure hunt, a soap carving competition, or a scavenger hunt. A huge birthday cake with lots of candles sets the stage for the gift exchange. This gift exchange is determined a few days before the party. Each person draws a name out of a bowl and keeps it a secret. Then, during the party, everyone piles into cars and heads to town to shop for their person. There's a three-dollar limit for the gift, and it has to relate to the theme!

Wrapping these gifts involves everything from empty cereal boxes to newspaper comic strips.

A grandmother herself now, Mary reflects, "I'm not sure who had the most fun, but that day was full of anticipation, creativity, laughter, and drawing closer to each other. What a blessing it was then, and even now as it brings back happy memories and smiles."

Juanita and Arthur

Juanita and Arthur invited their grandchildren to spend a week at their home every summer. This week always coincided with their church's Bible school. The children loved going to the Bible school in the mornings, and this provided a program that Juanita and Arthur did not have to run! They spent afternoons doing field trips with the children, and over the years these trips became part of the tradition as the children enjoyed visiting the same special places with their grandparents. Three of their six grandchildren went every summer from the time they started kindergarten through fifth grade, when they "graduated" from Bible school.

A favorite memory from a granddaughter: "Every day Granddaddy picked us all up from Bible school. 'Nanny' helped at church with Bible school during the morning, so Granddaddy would have our lunches all made and ready for us when we got home. I loved how he would cut the sandwiches for us into triangles and take the crust off for us (which my mom refused to do)! I thought those sandwiches were delicious, and I have never tasted anything like them!"

Juanita and Arthur's daughter Martha said, "Because my parents made time for my daughters when they were young, my parents and my daughters (who are now in college and grad school) have a direct relationship with each other that is not dependent on me. My daughters will happily call, text, or visit their grandparents on their own initiative."

Jesse and Nora

Jesse and Nora have four biological children and one foster daughter. While most of their grandchildren are small, their foster daughter's two sons are quite a bit older. These boys have grown up in a single-parent family and they are biracial. There have been many challenges, but Jesse and Nora have chosen to be intentional grandparents with these two boys. When the boys were preteens, they took each of them on their own trip to celebrate their launch into the teen years. They had a blast, but they also spent time in purposeful discussion during breakfast. They have found it easier to get kids to respond early in the day rather than waiting until evening. Jesse and Nora knew that these boys did not have anyone else who was likely to engage them in serious conversations. They asked questions that fell into several categories: manhood, faith, family, girls/dating/sex, and friends. Questions included, What does it mean to be a man? What words would you like to be used by others to describe you? Why is self-control so important? Where do you think you need to exercise self-control? How do you earn trust? What do you need most from me and your grandmother? What does a healthy relationship with a girl look like? What questions do you have about sex, or about pornography?

As a graduation gift, they recently took the eldest grandson to Washington, DC. A highlight on this trip was a visit to the Black History Museum. This setting provided a natural opportunity to discuss race. Their grandson felt impacted by being raised by a single Caucasian mom while having limited time with his African dad.

Each morning he had to come up with a question for Jesse and Nora. Some he chose were, How did you two meet each other? How did you know you were right for each other? Tell me why you started your business. What do you think is my greatest strength and weakness?

Although they shared Scripture with him, they were careful to listen and discuss and not to preach. They told him that there was no question that would make them love him less and provided a safe place for him to ask questions. They reminded him again and again of their unconditional love for him.

Creating thoughtful questions for these special times with older grandkids is one way to go deeper in our relationships with them.

Lisa

In 1929, an extended family gathered in a park pavilion to eat, visit, and worship. Someone decided they should organize, so they nominated a president, secretary, and treasurer. This group met for ninety years on the third Sunday in August at a park, a fire hall, or a church pavilion. It was only canceled once, during World War II.

How does a reunion last for ninety years? The first forty were led by Lisa's Aunt Eddie, the matriarch of the family. No one could say no to her. She was also a comic, and hearing her dramatic reading was worth the trip. Family lore says she was also chased from the outhouse by a swarm of bees in the late 1960s. This incident resulted in a change of venue. Lisa's mother took over as cheerleader and arm-twister in the 1970s.

Sixty to one hundred family members came for the food, which was traditional and plentiful: fried chicken (not from a bucket), macaroni and cheese (not from a box), applesauce (not from a jar), potato salad (not from a deli), country cured ham, iced tea, ice cream bars, and creamsicles. Family members contributed their favorite dishes. Each year their program included a talent show, a worship service (including Scripture readings, a sermon, and hymn singing), and prizes. The highlight for many was the singing of "Faith of Our Fathers" and "Blessed Be the Tie That Binds." They gave prizes to the oldest man and woman, the longest married couple, the youngest child, the largest family in attendance, and the family that had traveled the farthest.

All of these activities were recorded in the secretary's minutes. Attendance was also taken, as well as an offering to pay for the park rental.

Although this reunion no longer occurs, it reminds their family of their roots and the values of extended family. It also gives a vision of what their own family may become.

Initiating Simple Gatherings

One of the principles that has become apparent as I've interviewed other people is that so often it's the little things that develop into traditions that make for happy memories.

For Abby it's a tablecloth.

Abby's grandparents hosted many reunions. Families came and went throughout several days, but one thing remained constant: a blue tablecloth. Each person was encouraged to write something or draw a little picture on the cloth. During the following year, Grandma embroidered those words and drawings in colorful threads. Today the cloth is almost covered, but the family still finds spots to add a new birthday or wedding or memory of some hilarious event. (If sewing is not your gift, use permanent markers in different colors!)

For Glenis it's state parks and hilarious skits.

Glenis's seven aunts and uncles organize a reunion every other year. They alternate locations to make it easier for families to come. They have found state parks with camping and cabins to be great options. Various relatives take turns writing creative skits and hosting unique meals. Different generations participate in leading and creating the fun interactions.

For Peggy it's a service project.

Peggy has only one living cousin, but her four siblings and their spouses and children make up for this generational lack. For many years, family reunions centered around the memorable Christmas gatherings at her parents' home. As her parents grew older, it became harder to host their growing families. The longing for more shared experiences was satisfied when three of her siblings, their spouses, and their teenage children gathered in Wisconsin at a neglected house Peggy's family had inherited. Their vision was to bring the family together around something constructive. Sawing and chopping trees, hauling brush to burn piles, sharing one shower with twelve people, and cooking meals served to bond the reunion. But it wasn't all work. Having huge bonfires, roasting marshmallows, making homemade ice cream, and playing cards and charades made for a unique reunion. The whole family now loves returning to the house to enjoy the fruits of their labor.

Peggy relates, "I love the combination of people and purpose."

For Jerry and Nancy it's giving their own kids a break.

As parents of four kids, Jerry and Nancy remember how exhausting the early parenting years can be and how hard it can be for a young couple to have time alone. One of their goals is to do all they can to support the marriages of their kids. Recently they took their toddler grandkids for two nights and three days so the parents could have a break and time to focus on one another as a couple.

Nancy says, "It wasn't a real camp. They are too little. Most of our time was spent watching them chase each other, distracting them so they would not miss their mommies, and reading very short stories. To say we were exhausted at the end is an understatement. But we had the thrill of watching little ones bond, and it gave us dreams for the future."

For Babs it's a deck of cards.

Babs comes from a large family. It's hard to know who's who! Little children can feel overwhelmed even before they arrive. So Babs's niece created a unique deck of cards. Before the reunion, she got photos of each individual and each family unit. Today's social media world makes this easy to do. She had the pictures printed in 3 x 5 size, then had an office supply store (their laminators offer superior quality) laminate the cards. The children and adults love playing with the cards and guessing who belonged to each family!

Babs and her sister also made a collage of pictures of each family unit for an elderly aunt. Laminating two pictures back to back in one sheet made it very affordable. Many wonderful days have been spent with this aunt looking at these pictures, which she keeps on her bedside table.

For the Nelsons it's productions.

John comes from a big family. To build bonds, his parents have hosted a reunion every summer at their home in Maine. If a family misses one summer, they know they have next summer to look forward to.

Each year the cousins create dramas and perform them with costumes and props gathered from around the house or made with cardboard and markers. These productions develop leadership skills, lessen the fear of speaking before an audience, encourage storytelling and writing, and teach cooperation among siblings. The cousins do it all, and the parents get to sit back, laugh, and be entertained.

One older cousin reflects, "I always enjoyed that we got to have 'sleepovers' with one another instead of having to stay separately within individual families. A lot of the inspiration for our plays came from talking late at night, and we also had the chance to get to know one another on a deeper level. This small but repeated experience has built a bond that helps me to trust my cousins even though I don't see them all the time. I know that they would be there if I ever needed anything."

For Sarah it's honoring a military heritage.

Because Sarah's large extended family has lots of military connections, she decided to incorporate a military theme into a family reunion. Each person received an invitation to "Mission Impossible: Band of Cousins." On the cover was a WWII photo of her grandfather with his two brothers (triplets!) on a tank.

Everyone came dressed in camo, and the activities had different battle themes. Sarah put together a family military booklet for the children filled with short stories and pictures. Activities included an obstacle course, stories from military and family historians, games and water gun fights, and of course medals! At the end of camp, character awards were given out to the campers. The message: *character is what matters most.*

Your camp doesn't need to be fancy, expensive, or filled with big outings. Laughter and memories are found more often in the little things, even the spontaneous, unplanned things that occur. Nature and creation provide endless opportunities for games, intentional lessons, and the cultivation of awe and thanksgiving at what God has provided for our enjoyment.

Questions to Consider

1. What did you read above that you particularly liked? Remember to circle or underline things that might be helpful to you. Record these here and transfer them to your notes in chapter 5.

---

2. Do you know of other families who have hosted different types of camps or reunions? What have you learned from them? What worked and what didn't?

3. Now that you have finished eight chapters, what are your top three to five takeaways?

nine

Prayer:
The Best Thing
We Can Do for Our Family

An older Southern woman trying to encourage an extremely frustrated young mother exclaimed, "Honey, I knows you jus' wants to 'do for your chile.' That's natural. God made us like that."

We do want to "do" for our children. Just like God wanted to "do" for His children, Adam and Eve, back in the garden. For them He created the best of the best. The most beautiful surroundings in the world. He delighted in them. He enjoyed them. He provided for them—everything they would need. And yet it wasn't enough for them. I wonder how He felt. Disappointed? Yes, God has emotions. But also resolve. He knew the future, and it was going to be good.

When we hold our baby, our mother's heart kicks in. A heart that wants to protect, provide, and care for. We don't have to churn up love; it simply comes, and it grows and grows. Sometimes it's awkward at first. And after a stretch of sleepless nights we might just want to give our baby to someone else for a few days. We are exhausted. That's normal. But underneath the frustration is a parent's heart that cannot help but love. Just as God cannot help but love you and me, His precious children.

Neither you nor I are God, so our love, although strong, is not perfect. Whereas God's love for us is unconditional, ours for a child or grandchild or family member is sometimes conditional. We are selfish, imperfect, and needy. God is not shocked by this. He knows we are but dust (Ps. 103). He knows we need forgiveness and the power of the Holy Spirit, both of which He provides in abundance when we ask Him. He knows we are going to fail at this parenting thing, but He has the power to forgive and to redeem.

Every mother will feel like she has ruined her child—many times—at different ages. It's important to remember that *your ability to ruin your child is not nearly as great as God's power to redeem them.*

We do our best to raise our kids in Christ, teach them to love one another, equip them with character and life skills, meet their emotional needs, and provide the best education, the "right" connections, food, and clothing. We want them to succeed and mature into healthy adults who will make a positive contribution to society.

And, of course, we fail. Many times, over and over.

But there is one thing we can't fail at: prayer.

Prayer

Prayer is both simple and profound. God loves it when we come to Him in prayer. No matter how badly we have behaved, regardless of our prideful or wicked thoughts, He simply says, *Come.*

Come to me, all you who are weary and burdened, and I will give you rest. Take my yoke upon you and learn from me, for I am gentle and humble in heart, and you will find rest for your souls. For my yoke is easy and my burden is light. (Matt. 11:28–30)

Notice He does not say, "Come you who are super-spiritual, have kids who turned out right, exhibit perfect behavior, love your neighbor successfully, and succeed in your career."

No, it's just the opposite. God loves a broken and contrite heart (Ps. 51:17). I think this is why he called David "a man after my own heart" (Acts 13:22). It certainly wasn't because of David's behavior. He committed adultery and murder, among other sins. He even ran from God. Yet he also returned, over and over again. He kept coming to God in the midst of his messes. He had an intimacy with his heavenly Father that allowed the freedom of total transparency. There was nothing to hide. He realized that God already knew all of his junk. I love the psalms because David is so honest. Of course, there's some self-denial in there too. But he was a man after God's own heart because he shared his heart with God. And God loves deep transparency and intimacy with us.

It is in prayer that we come to a deep place of intimacy with our heavenly Father. We can be completely honest with Him. He already knows what is on our heart (Ps. 139). He delights in us (35:27). He loves it when we come to Him in need. I believe He especially loves it when we come to Him on behalf of our family members.

How Do We Begin to Pray for Our Families?

Begin with Hope

My friend Bel grew up with a mom who was unable to show empathy. Her mother's mom had died when she was four. As a result, Bel's mother was severely depressed, unpredictable, passive, and helpless most of Bel's life. To make matters worse, Bel's dad drowned when she was two. She struggled, growing up in a home with a depressed single mother. At the age of twelve she came to know Jesus Christ. She married; however, her husband walked out, leaving her with two daughters, ages one and three.

Bel sought out a Christian community and counseling. She did not give up. In time God brought her a wonderful godly husband. Today her girls are grown and she's a grandmother. Bel worked through the pain of her relationship with her mother, and they had some sweet years before her mother died. Bel says you must face the pain and work through it, but it is worth it to begin a new legacy for your family.

Bel's story reminds us: *No matter what you come from, you can be the first generation of a healthy family.*

Our God loves to redeem. He loves to do a new thing.

> I waited patiently for the LORD;
>   he turned to me and heard my cry.
> He lifted me out of the slimy pit,
>   out of the mud and mire;
> he set my feet on a rock
>   and gave me a firm place to stand.
> He put a new song in my mouth,
>   a hymn of praise to our God.
> Many will see and fear the LORD
>   and put their trust in him.
>   (Ps. 40:1–3)

For nothing will be impossible for God. (Luke 1:37 ESV)

There is always hope.

There have been many grandmothers who have impacted generations to come by their prayers. As the eldest grandchild in my mother's family, I was very close to my grandmother. She was a woman of prayer. I still picture her curled up in her bed in a lovely satin nightgown, gray hair spread over her pillow, bobby pins left on the floor. Her bed was covered with worn-out notes, several devotionals, and a falling-apart Bible. Many mornings I would tiptoe in and curl up beside her, and with the excitement of a little child, she would show me a verse that she had just read. I know she prayed for me and for my children. Her prayers have made a bigger difference than she could ever have imagined.

Begin with Assurance

God wants us to come to Him with assurance. Whenever, whatever we pray, we can know that He hears and that He will answer (Jer. 33:3; Heb. 4:16).

I have found it helpful to consider that, generally speaking, God answers prayer in three basic ways: "Yes," "No," and "Wait." He always answers out of love. Sometimes we ask for something that is not good for us. He may answer no. We don't understand, but we rest on the fact that it's a "love no." We see only in part. He has the whole picture. Often, He answers yes. Sometimes He answers wait, and the wait may feel like a deafening silence.

We wonder, *Is He there?* He is.

Does He care? He does.

In times of waiting, I call on Jeremiah's advice (Jer. 33:3). I ask Him to reveal to me something other, something different, than the issue at hand. I open myself to hearing something new, something special.

Isaiah reminds us,

> "For my thoughts are not your thoughts,
> neither are your ways my ways,"
> declares the LORD.

"As the heavens are higher than the earth,
so are my ways higher than your ways
and my thoughts than your thoughts." (Isa. 55:8–9)

God does answer. He always does what is best, not necessarily what is fast. And He is always working while we are waiting. Right now, as I write this, it's an ugly, bleak, and cold winter's day. On the surface it doesn't appear that anything is going on. But underneath the muddy ground God is preparing for a beautiful spring. Beauty will burst forth at just the right time. We can count on Him.

Begin with a Simple Plan

Often, when we think about praying, we just feel overwhelmed. There are so many needs. We don't even know where to begin. We read books on how to pray and feel guilty. We think, *I'll get to it someday when life calms down.* But life doesn't calm down. It just gets more complicated.

Perhaps we need a simple plan. A way to start small. I made myself a prayer notebook that I divided into seven sections, one for each day of the week. Each day has a theme and one general prayer that I pray for John and me and our kids and grandkids. I have additional notes for each day of the week. These are always evolving. Sundays my notebook is reserved for praise. It's the Sabbath, and I want to focus on God rather than people. This refreshes me. This Sunday section is blank. Yes, blank. This forces me to be creative in my praises.

There is no one right way to pray. Each of us is different. However, to encourage you, here are my daily prayers, straight from my teastained, messy prayer journal.

As you read the above, you probably noticed a lack of organization, repetition, and an uneven template. Talking with our Father is not meant to be organized or clean or perfect. It's meant to be real.

My Own Prayer Journal

Monday

Theme: Our relationship with God
Note: We have five children, all married, so we really have ten children. I pray this great prayer that Jesus taught His disciples (Matt. 6:9–13). I insert our initials into each phrase to personalize it. I have also added words of interpretation to enrich my prayer. I pray each phrase very slowly, usually out loud, to help me stay focused.

Our Father who art in heaven, hallowed be Your name. Your kingdom come; Your will be done (*in* [insert specific names]) *on earth as it is in heaven.*

Give us (repeat names above) *this day our daily bread* (a sense of Your provision, Your Holy Spirit, Your joy, Your presence, Your protection, Your intervention, Your leading).

Forgive us (repeat names) *our sins* (convict us, make our hearts tender so we would repent) *as we forgive those who have sinned against us.* (Help us to do this, to grant grace in our marriages).

Lead us (repeat names) *not into temptation* (help us to recognize evil and run from it, to call on Your power to defeat Satan) *but deliver us from evil.*

For Yours is the KINGDOM,
    the POWER,
        and the GLORY
forever and ever. Amen!

Tuesday

Theme: Our marriages
Note: This can be adjusted for singles. Single people can pray for their future mates, if God should choose for them to marry. Even if they do not feel the call to be married, they can pray for the married members of their family and friends, and for wisdom regarding how to support those marriages.

Dear Father,

You have called us into marriage. It was Your creation that You might be glorified. Lord, please be protecting our unions.

Give to each of us:
- *sweetness of speech*
- *a desire to work through struggles and stick to it when we are tempted to flee*
- *help in really listening and considering the other's view and not presuming; we want good communication*
- *eyes only for each other*
- *a desire to serve the other*
- *the discipline to quickly forgive and ask forgiveness*
- *a sense of how we are fitting together—two being better than one*
- *growing thankfulness for one another*
- *the discipline and time to pray together*
- *more spontaneous laughter*
- *growing tenderness*

Deliver us from:
- *taking one another for granted*
- *failing to appreciate or build up*
- *those who would tear apart our marriages*
- *wandering eyes*
- *emotional divorce*

And give us eyes to recognize how the enemy might try to tear us apart.

Please be adding layers and layers of glue into our unions and melting us into oneness.

May our marriages glorify YOU. Amen.

Wednesday

Theme: Our friendships

Note: This can be adjusted to include names of specific friends.

Dear Father,

You have created us for relationship with You, with our spouses, and with others. Even You had the twelve disciples and three best friends, Peter, James, and John. Father, I ask that You make each of us and our kids "There you are" people instead of "Here I am" people. Make us a people who care for others rather than expect others to cater to us.

I ask that You give all of our family members wise discernment today:

- to make time for You our first priority
- to recognize the enemy and how he attacks us individually
- to distinguish truth from falsehood in our emotions and our thoughts, and in what we hear
- to know what to say yes to and what to say no to
- in choosing the right company
- in parenting decisions
- in job decisions
- in housing decisions
- in financial decisions, and make us overly generous—down through all our generations
- in calendar decisions
- in words as we interact with others
- in handling the internet, phones, and other devices

Please also give to each of us:

- close believing friends who will hold us accountable and with whom we can raise our kids and commit to finishing the race without equivocating
- a few same-sex friends with whom we can be completely honest and pray together
- wisdom (James 1:5)

Amen.

Thursday

Theme: Boldness

Note: This layout is different. Prayer does not have to be neat or standard.

Father,

Please make all of us bold, much bolder than we are in sharing You. Give us conviction, character, and courage to proclaim You. Show my kids how to impart this to their kids. I ask that You give the "gift of *evangelism" to many of my grandchildren. Use all of our generations yet to come to bring many people to You.*

"When I called, you answered me; you greatly emboldened me." (Ps. 138:3)

Empower us with confidence in You and the courage to proclaim You with grace and humility in a hostile world. Amen.

Friday

Theme: "Heart for the world" day
Note: Put a world map up in your home and ask God to lead you to a certain people group or mission around the world for whom you can pray.

Broaden our hearts, O Lord; give us and our kids and grandkids a passion for the world and a passion for the poor, lonely, and hurting. Help us to notice those in front of us and listen to Your whispers to pray for one another, Your prompting to help someone else. Help us get out of our comfort zones, to know what is going on elsewhere, to expose ourselves and our kids to those not like us, to care for the widows and orphans.

Give us love, Father, for our own neighborhoods, cities, and countries. Show us a specific place in the world to "adopt." A special place to pray for, to care for. Give us a family vision.

Grow in our kids and grandkids a commitment to each other, to being together, to communicating. Father, they have so many demands of their own. Help them not to neglect each other but to strive to be together, to stay in touch, to show up when needed, to support one another financially, and to pray for one another. Amen.

Saturday

Theme: Extended family
Note: Focus on extended families (siblings, their kids, and their grandkids). Write down current needs as you learn of them. There are always needs, and it's a privilege to pray for one another.

Sunday

Theme: Praise day
(*Blank*)

Crucial Things to Remember

Prayer Is Always Evolving

My son Chris and his wife, Christy, have four children. Every year Christy sends four emails to her parents, to John and me, and to the children's godparents. Each email coincides with a child's birthday. She shares a brief update on the child from the past year and then gives us specific things to pray for in the coming year. For example: a contentious relationship with a sibling, more kindness, a deepening relationship with a parent, or a growing positive spirit rather than a negative one. And there are always thanksgivings, such as for improvement in pronunciation or for new friends in a new school. I paste these emails into my journal so I will know how to pray specifically for each child.

Sometime during the month of August, John and I email all of our kids, asking them to send us their prayer requests for themselves and each of their children for the coming year. I put these in my prayer journal as well and assign a day each week to one particular family. This keeps me from being overwhelmed and guides my prayer life.

Prayer Is Not All Up to Us

One of the greatest things we can do for our family and our friends is to pray for them. We are not meant to walk through this life alone. We need each other. As it says in Proverbs, "As iron sharpens iron, so one person sharpens another" (Prov. 27:17). Having a few friends who know you well and who will pray for you is a necessity, not a luxury. Moses had Aaron and Hur, David had Jonathan, Paul had Silas and Barnabas. Even Jesus had Peter, James, and John. Sometimes we need to carry a friend's burden or have someone carry ours.

I remember a time when I was struggling with an unreasonable fear about something. I found myself praying continuously throughout each day for God's peace. But it did not come. Finally, I told a close friend about this dilemma. My friend responded, "Susan, stop praying about this. I am taking this on for you, and I will pray every day for the next thirty days for this issue. You are to leave it on my shoulders. I will carry it." Handing this issue over to a friend brought me genuine freedom. We need friends.

It is easy to think too much about our issues. Even praying about them can cause them to grow in our heads. We try to churn up trust and it doesn't work. I have come to realize how easy it is to let our issue—whatever it is at the moment—become bigger in our heads than our God. We need an enlarged picture of how big our God is. This is the theme of my book *Risky Faith: Becoming Brave Enough to Believe the God Who Is Bigger Than Your World* (Loyal Arts Media, 2016).

I remember once, in a difficult season with a child, feeling so alone. I was praying and praying, but feelings of inadequacy flooded my heart. I felt that it was all up to me. And then I discovered Hebrews 7:25 and Romans 8:34. These verses basically state that Jesus is sitting at the right hand of God praying for us and our children *right now*. His job in heaven is to intercede for us. It's not all up to us! Right at this moment He is praying for my child and yours. What a relief!

Prayer Is One Thing at Which We Cannot Fail

There is not one way to pray, one set of words that is best, one pat formula. God looks at our hearts. He longs to hear our requests. It delights Him when we come to Him. No matter what.

Imagine a four-year-old child. This child has been disobedient. He has been punished and it's over, but all in all it's been, in the words of children's author Judith Viorst, a "terrible, horrible, no good very bad day," for the parent and the child. Your dejected child peeks around the corner into the room where you are curled up in your favorite chair, the family "cuddling chair." His little lip is quivering as he looks at you. He wonders, *Will I be received?*

What is your response as you look at his broken and contrite heart? Is it, *Don't come to me until you promise you will never do that again,* or *Don't come until you clean up your act,* or *Don't come until . . . ?* No, that would not be your response as you look at your brokenhearted toddler. Your arms would reach out, beckoning him into your lap. Your response would most likely be, *Come, child. Come. It's all right.*

If we in our imperfect love would respond in this manner, how much more is our heavenly Father in His perfect love responding to us with open arms, saying, *Come, come, my precious child. It is all right. Just come to Me.*

Father, we come. We come—single, married, young, old, in every condition. On behalf of our families, we come to You, the One who knows and loves each person in our family far more than we do.

"As for me, this is my covenant with them," says the Lord. "My Spirit, who is on you, will not depart from you, and my words I have put in your mouth will always be on your lips, on the lips of your children and on the lips of their descendants—from this time on and forever," says the Lord. (Isa. 59:21)

Appendix

In this section you will find examples, photos, and lists that we have talked about in each chapter. I hope they will give you a visual picture of what our camp or reunion is like. You can get an even better picture by viewing some of our homemade film clips at my website, https://www.susanalexanderyates.com/cousincamp/.

Under some items I explain *the why* of the item as well as *the what*. It is often helpful to know why we do what we do.

Worksheet for Children's Needs

To help ensure that what we do at camp meets the real needs of our grandchildren, we list the names of each camper coming and write out their needs as best we can, taking into consideration five areas of growth: *emotional*, *social*, *physical*, *spiritual*, and *mental*. Do not worry if you don't have something for each category. Some overlap. And every blank does not need to be filled in. Some you will think of in the moment. The goal is to plan a program that reflects the real needs of the kids, not merely plan a program. The needs change year to year. (A fuller explanation of this way of thinking is found in chapter 2.)

Sample Worksheet for Observing the Needs of the Grandchildren

Name (age)	Needs	Goals	Program
	Emotional		
	Social		
	Physical		
	Spiritual		
	Mental		
	Emotional		
	Social		
	Physical		
	Spiritual		
	Mental		
	Emotional		
	Social		
	Physical		
	Spiritual		
	Mental		

The Why

Using a worksheet like this helps us focus on real needs of those attending camp, instead of simply planning an event. The needs change year to year.

The What

This worksheet is one example of assessing the needs of those attending the event.

Consider this a working document. You will want to make changes throughout camp as needed. After camp is over, it is fun to look back at this to notice what worked (or didn't) and to jot down notes for next year. The purpose of this exercise is to establish a new way of thinking, not to see perfection.

"Praying Together for Your Children Builds Your Marriage" Blog Post

A few years ago, I wrote a post on my blog, *Susan Alexander Yates*, about the intersection between praying for our children and the health of our marriage. The full text of that post is below.

The Why

The best thing we can do for our marriage and for our kids is to pray for them.

The What

In this blog post I explain how praying together for our children has strengthened our marriage.

Praying Together for Your Children Builds Your Marriage

Years ago, John and I began an end-of-summer tradition of praying together for our children that helped us move into the fall with vision, unity, and clarity in how to parent our five kids. We designated a block of time alone (an overnight was the best!) to discuss each of our kids in five areas of growth: spiritual, emotional, mental, physical, and social.

We asked ourselves questions like:

- How is this child doing spiritually? Can we begin to encourage personal Bible reading or teach him how to keep a personal prayer list? (spiritual)
- Does a child need more discipline in study habits? How can we ensure this happens? (mental)
- Does one child need a close friend? (social)
- How about better eating habits? (physical)
- Is there a particular child that we feel isn't getting enough attention from us or is struggling with his self-image? (emotional)

As we talked about each child, we wrote down what we perceived to be their needs for the coming year and any goals that we might have. These lists became our individual prayer lists for each child.

The children did not know what we were praying.

One of the surprising blessings of this tradition was its impact on our marriage.

Simply taking time to discuss each child together enabled us to be on the same page with regard to that child. One of us often articulated something about a child the other had not noticed. Because we did this at the end of each summer, we had usually had some family vacation time together so that we both felt more in touch with each child.

As the mom, I found this drew me closer to John because it was easy to feel like "I do the kids and he does work." I know that's not true, but sometimes it sure did feel like it! This exercise always made me feel more like we were partners in parenting. After we discussed each child, we spent time praying together for that specific child's needs.

The year our son Chris was eleven, I felt that an emotional need for him was to "feel special." He was caught in the middle of four siblings, and I was concerned that he needed to be assured of how special he was. And so, we began to pray that he would feel special.

Halfway through the year he had an accident and fractured his skull. His brain was swelling, and the neurosurgeon really did not know how things would turn out. We were in the hospital for two weeks.

On the first day John and I began to pray that God would use this for good in our lives and particularly in Chris's life. Once he regained consciousness, we shared Romans 8:28 with him and prayed together. During the hospital stay, many people sent cards, came and visited, and prayed for him. We covered the walls of his hospital room with these love notes.

Just before he was released, I asked, "Chris, can you think of any way God has used this for good in your life yet?"

As he looked at the walls of his room covered with cards, he responded, "Wow, Mom, I didn't know how special I was."

Yes, God answers our prayers!

(Chris had no idea what was on our prayer list.)

We continued this "needs and goals" tradition every August throughout the years of raising our kids. When they reached college age, we shared the idea with them. We asked each child to email us and their siblings their own needs and goals—using these five areas of growth as a guideline—for the coming year so that we could pray for each other. John and I sent each of ours to them as well. Of course, they groaned, but they did it!

Today those old emails are still a reminder to me of God's faithfulness. Now that the kids are grown, we take turns sharing needs and goals at adult dinners during our family week together in the summer. This gives us specific insights into each other's lives, and as we pray for one another in the following months we are drawn closer together as a family.

Susan Alexander Yates "Praying Together for Your Children Builds Your Marriage," *Susan Alexander Yates* (blog), August 25, 2014, https://www.susan alexanderyates.com/praying-together-for-your-children-builds-your-marriage/.

--------- **The Plan of Salvation** ---------

The Why

Often, we don't know how to simply explain the gospel. Children aren't asking deep theological questions. Those will come later. But we all need to know how to explain the gospel in a simple manner.

The What

Here is how John and I explain God's plan of salvation.

The Best Thing in All the World

Introduction

Ask: Do you know what's the best thing in all the world? (Let them give answers, then explain.)

It's living every day of your life just the way God created you to live!

God made you, He loves you, and He wants to lead you into all that He has planned for you.

Scripture

The Bible says:

See what great love the Father has lavished on us, that we should be called the children of God! (1 John 3:1)

Ask: What do you think *lavish* means? (Let them respond, then explain.)

God sent His Son Jesus from heaven to bring us the Father's love, to show us how to live, and to help us become close to God.

Jesus answered, "I am the way and the truth and the life. No one comes to the Father except through me." (John 14:6)

Even when bad men killed Him, Jesus rose from the dead. He will never die.

The Bible says:

Wicked men . . . put him to death by nailing him to the cross. But God raised him from the dead, freeing him from the agony of death, because it was impossible for death to keep its hold on him. (Acts 2:23–24)

All of us have done things and said things and thought things that are very wrong, but if we ask God to forgive us, He will, and Jesus will come to be with us all our life when we ask Him to.

The Bible says:

If we confess our sins, [God] is faithful and just and will forgive us our sins. (1 John 1:9)

Jesus said:

Here I am! I stand at the door [meaning the door of our heart] and knock. If anyone hears my voice and opens the door, I will come in. (Rev. 3:20)

Never will I leave you; never will I forsake you. (Heb. 13:5)

I am with you always. (Matt. 28:20)

Ask: How long will Jesus stay with you? (Wait for answers, then explain.)

This is the greatest thing in the world, to know that Jesus is always with us and will always help us.

Ask: Would you like to ask Jesus to come into your life and always be with you?

You can right now.

You can pray with me. I will say a sentence, then you repeat it.

Prayer

Dear God,

Thank You for creating me and loving me. I ask You to come into my heart right now. Please forgive me for all that I have done that I should not have done. Help me live my life for You. Thank You.

In Jesus's name. Amen.

When we ask Jesus to come into our life, He does! He will always be with you. As you grow to know Him and love Him, He will guide you, and when you die you will be in heaven with Him, which is the very best of all.

——— Assurance Letter ———

The Why

We want our kids to have complete assurance that they know Jesus. We don't want them to hope or wonder.

The What

We wrote this sheet to be a reminder of what occurs when we give our lives to Christ. It is helpful for anyone. We paste it into the back of each child's journal.

Dear grandchildren,

We have prayed for each of you since we learned you were to be born, and God has made you perfectly from the beginning. "I am wonderfully made" (Ps. 139).

We pray many things for you, but most important to us is that you come to know Jesus, whom God sent for us so that we could become His very own children. Your parents had you baptized, and they and your godparents, and everyone else who loves you, promised that they would do all they could to help you love and trust Jesus as your friend and Savior.

"For God so loved the world that he gave his one and only Son, that whoever believes in him shall not perish but have eternal life" (John 3:16).

"To all who did receive him, to those who believed in his name, he gave the right to become children of God" (John 1:12).

Jesus comes to us and knocks on the door of our very own life, and if we open the door in faith and ask Him, He comes into our life, and He will not leave us.

"Here I am! I stand at the door and knock. If anyone hears my voice and opens the door, I will come in and eat with that person, and they with me" (Rev. 3:20).

"Never will I leave you; never will I forsake you" (Heb. 13:5).

When you asked Him to come into your life, He did!
When you asked Him to forgive your sins, He did!

"As far as the east is from the west, so far has he removed our transgressions from us" (Ps. 103:12).

Whenever you disobey God and you ask Him to forgive you, He will always forgive you.

"If we confess our sins, [God] is faithful and just and will forgive us our sins and purify us from all unrighteousness" (1 John 1:9).

You do not need to ask Him to come into your life more than once. He says to those who believe in Him, *"I am with you always"* (Matt. 28:20).

You can know that one day you will be in heaven with Him. Going to heaven isn't dependent on our being good enough to deserve it—no one is good enough to deserve heaven. This is a gift to those who have accepted that Christ died for their sins.

"God has given us eternal life, and this life is in his Son. Whoever has the Son has life" (1 John 5:11–12).

When Christ comes into your life, it is His Holy Spirit who comes and gives you the ability to live the life He has planned for you, and as you learn to depend on His help, you learn that Christ's Spirit in you is the key to enable you to live a life that pleases God. He intends that we depend upon Him for the strength we need, not upon ourselves.

"Since we live by the Spirit, let us keep in step with the Spirit" (Gal. 5:25).

You not only have a big family of cousins who love you and love Jesus but a great, large family of other brothers and sisters in Christ who will help you grow up in Him.

Just as all of us go through different physical growth stages, you will go through different stages in your spiritual growth. It's so important to have friends to whom you can go with your spiritual questions. There is no question, or doubt, or feeling that is silly or insignificant. And it really helps to have others who have "been there" to guide the way! You can always ask an older Christian any questions you have. They will be glad to help you.

"In him and through faith in him we may approach God with freedom and confidence" (Eph. 3:12).

We are so proud of you, and we love you so much!

Your Ghee and Poppy

Four Things You Can Know for Sure

The Why

Too often we lack the assurance that Christ is in our life. Perhaps we don't feel Him, or we've strayed from Him. His being in our life is not dependent on our feelings, which go up and down. Nor is it dependent on our behavior. He is always ready to forgive us. It is dependent on the facts—the promises He has made to us. We have to put our faith in the facts instead of in our feelings. This card is just one more reminder of this, and it's also handy for sharing with someone else. We laminated this for the kids to take home and keep in their Bibles.

FOUR THINGS YOU CAN KNOW FOR SURE

1. **JESUS LOVES YOU AND WANTS TO COME INTO YOUR LIFE.**
Jesus knocks on the door of your heart. If you open the door and ask him, he will come into your life and he will never leave you.
"Behold I stand at the door and knock. If anyone opens the door I will come into Him." (Rev. 3:20)
"I will not leave you or forsake you." (Hebrews 13:5)
"For God so loved the world that He gave his only son that whoever believes in him should not perish but have eternal life." (John 3:16)

2. **HE FORGIVES YOUR SINS.**
When you ask him to forgive your sins, He does!
"If we confess our sins God is faithful to forgive our sins and to cleanse us from all unrighteousness." (1 John1: 9.)
"As far as the east is from the west so far has he removed our sins from us." (Psalm 103)

3. **YOU CAN KNOW YOU WILL ONE DAY GO TO HEAVEN.**
Going to heaven isn't dependent on being good enough to deserve it- no one is good enough to deserve heaven. It is a gift to those who have accepted that Christ died for their sins and given themselves to God.
"God has given us eternal life and this life is in his son; whoever has the son has life. (I John 5:10-12)

4. **YOU HAVE THE HOLY SPIRIT TO HELP YOU LIVE THE CHRISTIAN LIFE.**
When Christ comes into your life, it is his Holy Spirit that comes in and gives you the power to live the life he has planned for you. He will give us the power to live. We can't do it on our own.
"If we live by the Spirit, let us also walk by the Spirit." (Galatians 5:25.)
You have a great, large family of other brothers and sisters in Christ who will help you grow up in Him.

────── **A Photo of Our Champion Wall** ──────

The Why

Kids like to see their names and remember who won what the year before. You'll see that we did not do this in the early camps.

The What

We made a simple trophy wall in our basement!

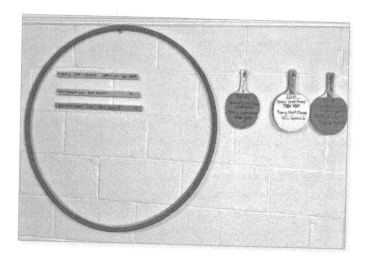

────── **"Raising Good Conversationalists" Blog Post** ──────

Not long ago, I wrote a post on my blog, *Susan Alexander Yates*, about teaching our children how to be good conversationalists. The full text of that post is below.

The Why

In today's social medial world, it's not easy for our kids (and sometimes us) to learn how to engage with another person face-to-face.

We feel awkward, don't know how to talk, or even how to carry on a conversation.

The What

We practice conversations at camp with the older kids.

Raising Good Conversationalists

Do you sometimes feel embarrassed in front of your friends because your child won't talk and simply grumbles a "yes" or "no" to an adult's questions? Do you have trouble getting him to talk? Do you yourself feel awkward engaging someone in a conversation?

Some skills in the family will be more "*caught than taught*," but becoming a good conversationalist is *not* one of them. In fact, very few things are simply caught. It takes both modeling *and* teaching to raise our kids into the adults God has called them to become.

Today's kids are less socially mature than in earlier generations. Technology has contributed to this. It's easier to engage a screen than to look someone in the eye and have a live conversation. However, a lack of teaching has also contributed to this. Many parents simply don't realize that conversing is an art form that requires training.

Training our kids to be good conversationalists is an example of living out the second great commandment: "Love your neighbor as yourself." One way of loving your neighbor (or any other person) is caring enough to draw them out in conversation—to demonstrate that you are really interested in their life, in their opinions, and in learning from them. We want to raise "other-centered kids" not "self-centered kids."

With spring vacation and Easter coming many of us will be with extended family and friends. This presents us with an excellent opportunity for teaching the art of conversation. Here are a few tips:

1. Shyness is not a valid excuse.

Some of us are extroverts. It's more natural for us to reach out, to be friendly, to engage with another. Others of us are introverts. We'd rather be left alone and not converse. We are shy to the core. However, shyness should not become an excuse for rudeness. We must not let a reticent child off the hook simply because he or she is shy. We will have to work harder with this child, and it may take longer but it is crucial in raising him or her to become an adult who reaches out to others and is also comfortable in any social situation. An extroverted child will present us with other challenges. He or she will need to learn it's not necessary to be the center of attention and how to encourage someone else. Each child can learn skills that will help him or her learn how to talk to others.

2. Think schedules and relationships.

It is helpful to think in terms of two categories: schedules and relationships. No matter what the age, everyone has a schedule, and everyone has relationships. Write down questions that fall into one of these categories. Ask a child, "What is your favorite part of your day at school?" (schedule question). Ask an adult, "Tell me about a project you are working on," or "What does a typical week look like for you?" (schedule question). Ask a child, "Who do you like to hang out with at school, or on weekends?" (relationship question). Ask an adult, "Looking back in your life, who has influenced you in a positive way and how?" (relationship question).

3. Learn to use the "clue-in."

My son John had invited his friend Joe to come over. I did not know Joe but I wanted to be able to engage with him.

So I asked John, "Son, I don't know Joe and I'd like to get to know him but I need you to *clue me in* to what he's like. What is he into? Sports, music, technology?"

"Mom," John replied, "he's into art and in fact he's really good at it but his parents don't understand him because they are into sports so it would be really cool if you could talk to him about art and maybe ask him to bring over some of his paintings to show you sometime."

I appreciated my son's *clueing me in* and I had a wonderful time getting to know Joe.

If you are going to be with others or are having others over for the holidays, tell your child about a guest and give them some specific questions they might be able to ask the guest. Sometimes it's helpful to do this together and to write the questions down, particularly if your children are young. We live in the DC area where folks are adept at creating "talking points." We need to do this with our kids. Often if we are going to an event my husband *clues me in* about someone I might meet and how I can engage him or her in conversation. I do the same for him. It helps make conversation less awkward and can be the beginning of a deep friendship. Most importantly, it makes the other person feel valued.

4. Create a list of good questions.

Sit down with your kids and come up with a list of good questions. You can use the categories of schedules and relationships as a framework but also make a written list of simple "Anyone-Anytime" questions. Here are a few to get you started: Who is one of your heroes in life? Why? What is one of your favorite books? If you could travel anywhere in the world, where would you like to go? What do you enjoy doing when you have some free time? If you could meet anyone in the world, who would it be? Why? What has been invented during your lifetime? What is one of your favorite hobbies? What was life like for you when you were my age? (This is a good one to ask a grandparent.) Have your children think of questions they would ask other kids (both older and younger) as well as other adults.

5. Prepare for a specific event.

Now it's time to try this out. Discuss an upcoming event. It might be a meal with other families or grandparents. Discuss the folks who will be there. *Clue one another in* as to something you know about several of the people attending. Select at least one question for each member of the family to use with someone they choose.

Their assignment: Ask a question of their person sometime during the event. After the event sit together and share what you found out. It works best if you make this a discovery game with younger kids. With older kids or adults simply make time to debrief and share the things you discovered about others. You may hit resistance with your kids, but do it anyway. The more they do it, the easier it will become.

6. Do it over and over again.

The first time you do this, even if you are simply doing it for yourself, will be the hardest. But anything that is new is awkward at first. Simply keep at it. Keep working on this with your children. Practice asking each other questions at family meals. Don't give in to weariness. It takes years for this to become natural for some of us. Often, we will not feel like caring for others. But we do it anyway because God has called us to reach out to others. *We don't live life by doing what we feel like but by doing what is right.*

I remember struggling for years to teach Allison, our first child, how to engage a guest at the dinner table. Most often she sat in stony silence the whole meal. I'll never forget the day we had her choir director over for a meal, and Allison asked her some questions about music. We watched, amazed as our daughter engaged her teacher. She laughed; she actually talked! Afterwards my husband and I looked at each other and said, "Whose child was that?" What happened? After years of repeated training, role playing, nagging, and feeling like failures as parents, we were finally seeing results. God is faithful even when we don't feel like we are making progress. He is at work in the lives of our children even when we can't see it. One day we will; meanwhile we keep at it and pray for small signs of progress to encourage us to keep on keeping on! Our God has unlimited patience.

Susan Alexander Yates, "Raising Good Conversationalists," *Susan Alexander Yates* (blog), originally published February 14, 2018, https://www.susan alexanderyates.com/raising-good-conversationalists/.

─── A Photo of the Cabinets ───
Covered with Everything

The Why

The kids will ask hundreds of questions about camp. We post this schedule and other information so we don't have to answer the same question over and over, and also to let them know what is coming next. (We have a private, more detailed one for us.)

The What

Simple sheets with lots of information about camp taped on our kitchen cabinets where everyone can see them. For small kids, tape them low.

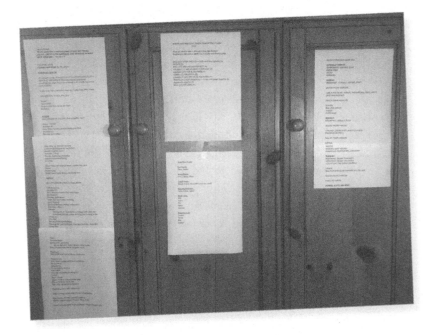

——— "Things to Do" List ———

The Why

We live in an age in which our children expect to be entertained. It is unusual for them to create their own entertainment (without devices). This can stifle creativity. Often a child will whine, "I'm bored! There's nothing to do!"

The What

In order to foster creativity and give our children ideas for individual play, we created a list to which the children have added their ideas. For years it has been displayed on our wall.

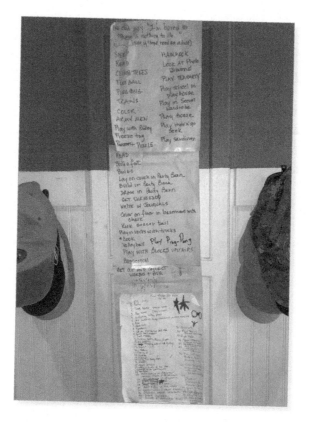

"Alexander Anecdotes" (Our Big Reunion Newsletter)

The Why

Getting together for a long weekend with family members that you haven't seen in a long time—and some you haven't even met—can be awkward in the beginning. *What will I talk to this person about? Who is this relative?* We wanted folks to come feeling a little bit up-to-date on one another and with a context for conversations.

The What

Several adult cousins created two editions of an "Alexander Anecdotes" newsletter. First, they emailed everyone coming and asked them to fill in a questionnaire. They also requested a photo of each person or family. This made up the first edition of the newsletter. The second edition contained answers from folks who had not replied to the first request. When they saw the first edition, they wanted in on the second! Both editions were sent out to everyone over email, and most of us printed them out to save in family files.

Here are some of our questions:

1. Each person entered two truths and a lie, and folks had to guess the answers!
2. Each person sent a photo of themselves with one-sentence answers to these questions:
   - Currently: (what I'm doing)
   - Looking forward to: (in the coming year)
   - Best purchase of the last year:
   - A nugget: (something I've liked)
   - A little revelation:
   - Passion:

3. Favorite things to watch (TV, movies), to read (books), to listen to (music).

Just reading these pages from years ago makes me laugh and rejoice again!

Additional Reading from Susan's Blog

Whenever I speak on "family," I am often asked about the relationships between mothers and adult daughters, as well as between mothers-in-law and daughters-in-law. Here are four blog posts on those topics that I hope will encourage you.

Mothers and Adult Daughters: Understanding One Another

Relationships between mothers and adult daughters can be such a source of joy, but also at times deeply challenging. This post is full of honest feedback from both sides, so we can understand each other better—and love each other well.

Recently a young mother said to me, "I realized how much I want to please my mother. I long to hear her say, 'You're a good mom. Your children are wonderful.'"

An older mother commented, "I wish my adult daughter would tell me some things I did in raising her that were good and helpful to her. Even though I'm the adult now, I still feel like I did so many things wrong in raising my daughter."

What I hear in both of these comments is the cry for approval.

We older moms long to know that we did and are doing some things right. We desperately want to please our adult daughters. And grown-up daughters want their mothers to admire them for what they're doing now.

Sometimes we mess up in trying to communicate our approval. We don't mean to do this. Both of us want to have a good relationship with each other. Yet often we don't understand one another, or we misjudge each other. Simply put, we don't know how to build a grace-based relationship.

What We Wish For

In an effort to understand what mothers and daughters long for, I asked some women what they wished their mother or daughter knew about them. Here are some responses.

From daughters: I wish my mom . . .

"I wish my mother knew how much I need to hear her say, 'You are doing such a good job as a mom.'"

"My mom and dad are always together. Sometimes I want my mom to myself."

"My mother is really great at doing things for us, but sometimes I wish she'd use words to say how much she loves me—words like: 'I love you,' 'I like who you are becoming,' or 'I'm proud of you.'"

"I wish my mom would share more of her heart with me, who she really is, not just Mom."

"I wish my mom would seek Jesus."

"I wish she would remember how hard it is to be a parent."

"I wish my mother talked less and asked me how I am more and then listened. Then I'd feel I could trust her more."

"I wish she would just listen to my thoughts and emotions rather than always jumping in to give me her thoughts or advice."

"I wish my mom would tell me that when I was little our home was not always perfectly clean. That would take the pressure off me to have a perfectly clean, decorated, organized home when she visits."

From moms: I wish my daughter . . .

"I wish she understood that even though I have an old body I still have feelings of inadequacy just like she does."

"I wish she knew how important Christ is in my life. She believes but doesn't seem to be growing in her faith."

"I wish she would let me know the inner world of her heart and that she would want to know mine."

"I wish my daughter would see me, would care to know who I am and who I am in the Lord. To know I want God's best for her, that I'm not just who you call for babysitting or to help out for her needs."

"I wish my adult daughter didn't have a vision of me as 'perfect.' I've shared my struggles with her, but she still thinks anything she does that's different from how I would have done it is wrong."

"My mother is in heaven now, but I wish she could know that all the effort she poured into me was not wasted and it fell on good soil."

Loving, Gracefully

So, what can we do to grow a grace-based relationship with one another?

1. Realize that because this relationship is so important to us, we are both fragile and unusually sensitive to one another.
2. Determine to grant grace by not taking offense at something said that was hurtful. Instead, respond with "I don't think you realize it, but when you said _____ it made me feel_____." (There's a good chance she had no idea.) Going further in this conversation might involve: "I am so sorry I made you feel that way. Tell me another way I could have put my comment." Remember, some comments are better left unsaid.

3. Keep in mind other factors. Look at the home in which your mother was raised. She may have wounds from her family of origin that have left a deficit in her ability to mother. Or your daughter may have wounds of which you are unaware.

4. Focus on and verbalize what the other does right. "It meant so much to me when you_____." Be as specific as possible. Occasionally do this in writing. Then it can be reread!

5. Learn each other's love language. Ask her what hers is! (Check out *The 5 Love Languages* by Gary Chapman.) Then love her in the way she needs, which may be very different from what you need.

6. Recognize that even though our longing for approval from each other is natural, our deeper longing is for our heavenly Father's approval. We can be assured of this.

"Therefore, there is now no condemnation for those who are in Christ Jesus" (Rom. 8:1).

Thankful Hearts

I also asked these women to tell me what they appreciated in their mothers or adult daughters. Here's what they said.

From daughters:

- "I'm thankful that my mom did not pressure me with worry when it became obvious that I wouldn't marry right away. I was struggling enough with singleness and her concern would have made it worse."

- "I'm thankful my mother is willing to do errands and go places with me when I'm home visiting her, and that she has begun to relate to me adult to adult. This was awkward at first but good for both of us."

- "I am thankful that she spends time with my kids, that she babysits and helps with all the doctor's appointments."

- "I am so thankful for my close relationship with my mother. Now that I'm an adult with my own family, my mom has truly become my confidant and friend."
- "My mom has a servant's heart and always encourages us to look at the positive side, no matter what."
- "I'm thankful that my mom makes a point to ask me how she can pray for me."

From older moms:

- "I'm thankful that my daughter continues to enjoy reminiscing about growing up and our experiences together."
- "I'm thankful that my daughter has always been there for me, especially since my husband died."
- "What I really appreciate about my daughter is that she is teachable."
- "My daughter is gracious and kind. She looks to my needs and has a gift of love."
- "I appreciate how my daughter loves others, puts the Lord first in her life, and turns to Him in times of waiting. She's more relational than I am."
- "I'm thankful for a daughter who loves her friends well."

I've learned some valuable tips from these honest comments. I hope you have as well. This is my prayer for each of us:

Lord, help us to focus on the good in our mothers and in our daughters. Enable us to overlook an offense—to choose to bless rather than to criticize. Show us tangible ways we can communicate love to them. Help us to assume the best of one another. And to believe that with you "nothing is impossible" (Luke 1:37).

Susan Alexander Yates, "Mothers and Adult Daughters: Understanding One Another," *Susan Alexander Yates* (blog), originally published May 8, 2019, https://www.susanalexanderyates.com/mothers-and-adult-daughters -understanding-one-another/.

Navigating the Holidays with
Parents, In-Laws, and Children

It's the season! I'd love to give you some simple tips for faithfully navigating the holidays.

Your head is likely spinning with preparations: shopping, cooking, invitations, fundraisers, holiday cards, and parties. And this is above and beyond the regular stuff on your plate: sports teams, concerts, work deadlines, school projects. (And does your child have yet another ear infection?)

For many there's another source of underlying stress—your in-laws or parents are coming for the holidays, or you are going to be with them!

You may be anticipating this visit with great joy or with a bit of dread, depending on your relationship with them. However, either way, simply having extra people around can add confusion and increase your stress levels.

Four tips will help make these holidays good for everyone.

1. Have realistic expectations.

It's easy to be swayed by the picture of a perfect family deeply enjoying one another by the fireside at Thanksgiving or Christmas. Our longing for this image can set us up for disappointment.

There is no perfect family. We are all sinful people. You and I are going to disappoint someone in our family this season. And someone is going to disappoint us.

It may be wise to discuss expectations before the visit. If you are the elder visiting your adult kids, don't go with your own plan as to how you will "help." What looks like help to you may not be what your kids call help. Instead say, "I'd love to help you in any way I can but you need to tell me exactly what that will look like for you." And this will be different for each one of your children's families.

If you are the children visiting with your kids, ask your elders for one or two specific things you can do to help them. After the visit, be sure your kids write a thank-you note to their grandparents. They often feel taken for granted. We all want to be appreciated. Thoughtfulness is a character trait we want to develop in our children, and thank-you notes provide one way to do this.

2. Guard against a critical spirit.

Your mother-in-law doesn't load the dishwasher the way you want her to, or messes up your wash, or doesn't pay enough attention to a specific child. It's easy to be critical of her, and criticism becomes resentment. Realize that her motive was to help. She may have gone about it in the wrong way, but at least she tried.

On the other side, you may be the older parent really disappointed by the fact that your children are letting your grandkids trash your house. They are not disciplining them as you think they should. And you feel unappreciated. Realize that your children are exhausted. The season of parenting little kids is one of the most stressful periods of life. Cut them some slack, especially in this season.

Holidays and family reunions are not the best time to deal with "issues." Issues are better dealt with during the year. Family reunions are times to celebrate what is good. The rest of the year is the time to nurture the relationships. At this season, choose to believe the best in one another.

3. Plan specific fun.

Plan one or two specific things to do together.

One of my greatest treasures is an old tape on which we recorded an interview we did with my elderly grandmother. We asked her what it was like to grow up in the deep South. (She was born in 1889!) We asked her what was invented while she was a child, what life was like for her parents and grandparents, toys she played with, who was president, what was happening in the world. It was fascinating, and today it is a part of our own grandchildren's history.

Maybe you want to do something similar and record an interview with your elders. Have your kids come up with some of the questions. This is their heritage, and one day they will appreciate it.

One family I know makes gingerbread houses. It's a multigenerational tradition and provides fun bonding for all.

4. Keep the main thing the main thing.

In today's world it's easy to let our family or the family we wish we were become an idol. If there are difficult relationships within our families we feel like failures. We look at another family, and they seem to have it all together, to be perfect. And ours isn't.

This pain becomes more pronounced during the holidays. This is normal, but we have to remember that our family is not the main issue nor should it be the central focus.

Thanksgiving is a time to be thankful to God for who He is and for what He has done.

Fill a bowl with corn kernels. Have each person take several kernels and share something they are thankful for as they place each one in an "offering" basket. Make a paper chain with children. Have them write one thing for which they are thankful on each strip, then add them to the chain and use it to decorate your home.

Christmas is about the birth of Jesus, who was born to die.

In fact, to die on the cross so that our sins might be forgiven. He knows we are broken. He knows not one single family is perfect. That's why He came. He came to bring healing for all.

No matter what type of family you come from there is good news: you can be the first of a generation of healthy families.

This season we need to keep our focus on Him. We need to ask Him to give us a grateful heart for what He has done for us and to ask Him for the insight to see things to be grateful for in each family member.

Susan Alexander Yates, "Navigating the Holidays with Parents, In-Laws, and Children," *Susan Alexander Yates* (blog), originally published November 7, 2018, https://www.susanalexanderyates.com/navigating-holidays-with-family/.

Mothers-in-Law and Daughters-in-Law: Women Share Their Hearts

Recently I posted a blog about being a mother-in-law. It generated a lot of response, so I decided to probe a little deeper and sent a questionnaire to a number of friends, both mothers and daughters. I was after honesty, and I got it!

I asked two questions and received a variety of answers.

If you are the mother-in-law: What do you wish your daughter-in-law knew about you?

- I wish she knew how badly I want a relationship with her and that I know I mess up sometimes.
- I wish she knew how frightened I am that she won't love or accept me and I will be locked out of a full relationship with her, my son, and grandchildren to come.
- Sometimes I worry that our relationship will be a formality and not true love.
- It can be hard for me when they spend most of their spare time with her family. It makes me feel unwanted.
- Sometimes I don't feel appreciated for all that I do. A thank-you note, a text, an email would be wonderful. (And I wish she'd teach their kids to do this as well.)
- I wish she'd call me simply to say, "How are you and how can I be praying for you?"
- I would love it if she initiated time with me.

If you are a daughter-in-law: What do you wish your mother-in-law knew about you?

- That I felt pressured by her to leave my job when I had our first baby. Her strong views made me feel like she didn't value what I felt in giving up my job.
- I want to trust that she will keep confidences that I share with her and not tell someone else.
- I want her to want to know me in adulthood and not always talk about her son when he was small but also about his life and mine now.
- I wish she knew how much I want a good relationship with her. I wish she'd call me by my name.
- I wish she would let me "be me" with my own history and not expect me to be like her.

- I wish she knew I am not competing with her. How she and I do things may be different but I am not competing.
- I need her appreciation and encouragement.
- I wish she'd let me help her and do things for her.

These are just a few of the responses, but what was surprising to me was how similar many of the responses were.

What I see is that both mothers-in-law and daughters-in-law long for good relationships.

With some family dysfunction this may not be possible, or it may take a very long time, but generally speaking it is the desire on both sides.

Unfortunately, our culture assumes that this relationship is difficult, contentious, and most often unpleasant. Pointed jokes produce laughter but also cause pain and create expectations for a difficult relationship. Expectations that may be false.

What if we understood that we are both sinful people in need of forgiveness? It's not because we are in-laws that we sometimes don't get along. It's because we are humans.

What if we began to speak about this relationship in positive terms?

What if instead of reacting we began to grant grace?

A thirty-two-year-old friend of mine put it this way:

I found the hardest hurdle for me was going from having a mother-in-law who felt more of "the other" to having a second mother. It took several years but somewhere along the line she stopped being my "in-law" and started to just be my family. I think the best thing you can do to have a healthy relationship with your mother-in-law is to really take the "what's yours is mine" part of marriage seriously and to really love her like you love your own mother. She is yours and that is precious. And from there we can remember that family doesn't always agree or get along but they always love each other, fight for each other, and take care of each other with a love like none other.

Whatever your relationship is like, it's most important to remember that God knows both of you intimately.

He knows our every thought (Ps. 139). He loves each of us unconditionally. He desires for our relationship with our in-law to be one of love and acceptance. He will use us to sharpen each other. He is in the process of growing both of us up into the women He has created us to be (Phil. 1:6). It will take time. We are impatient. He is not. Be encouraged!

Nothing is impossible for Him (Luke 1:37).

Susan Alexander Yates, "Mothers-in-Law and Daughters-in-Law: Women Share Their Hearts," *Susan Alexander Yates* (blog), originally published April 11, 2018, https://www.susanalexanderyates.com/mothers-in-law-and-daughters-in-law-women-share-their-hearts/

How to Be a Great Mother-in-Law

A great mother-in-law?

Okay, most days I'd settle for just being a good one or even just not messing up a relationship too badly. I've been a mother-in-law for twenty-three years now. We have five kids—three daughters and two sons. All of them are married, so I have both sons- and daughters-in-law. And the things I've learned over the years have come mostly from the mistakes I've made.

When our daughter Allison was a newlywed, she was about to drive overnight alone on a trip. "We don't want you to do that. It's too dangerous," we said. After further discussion, she came to us and said, "This is not really your decision. You have to let me and Will (her husband) decide what to do." As hard as it was, she was right.

Since I've been in the school of "in-lawing" for quite some time now, I thought I'd share with you five things I have learned from my own life, as well as from friends, which I hope will help you as you attend this "school" with me.

1. Our priorities change when our child gets married.

When our child marries the priority relationship is no longer our relationship with our child but their relationship with each other. The most important thing to me now is to cultivate their marriage. So when your newlywed daughter calls and says, "Mom, I am going to buy a couch. What kind should I get?" Your answer needs to be, "What does your husband think?" We have to step back from being the primary counselor to pushing them toward each other. God's Word describes marriage as to leave, to cleave, and to become one flesh. Many marriages run into trouble because either the husband or the wife does not "leave emotionally." We in-law parents can contribute to this problem by continuing to be too involved in our kids' lives. It's time to relinquish them to each other.

If possible, encourage your newlywed kids to live away from both sets of parents their first two years of marriage. Geographical distance will promote the emotional leaving and encourage the needed cleaving.

2. Be patient in building the relationship.

We want our families to be close. We want to have a deep friendship with our new son- or daughter-in-law. But sometimes we expect this to happen too quickly, and we can suffocate the new family member. If our expectation for an instant, close-knit family is too high we will be disappointed. It's important to remember that anything that is new is awkward. It is often hard for a new daughter-in-law to instantly embrace her new family. Give the new member some time to adjust. The first two years are likely to be a time of slowly grafting them into the family.

3. Focus on common interests.

We have to work patiently at building a relationship with a new in-law. Find out their interests and study the things that interest them. If they are "into" natural foods, study nutrition. If they are in business, try to learn about their field of business. Do things with them that they like. If they like fishing, go fishing. If they are readers, read what they read. Be interested in their life. Get to know their friends. However, remember there is a delicate balance between overwhelming them and ignoring them.

4. Ask your own child how you can love his or her spouse well.

Usually we want to love our in-law child but often we don't know how to go about it. Their love language may be completely different from ours.

(*The 5 Love Languages* by Gary Chapman is a good resource.) Ask your own child, "How can I love your spouse well this year? What can I do that would communicate love to him or her? Is there anything that I am doing that is offensive to them?"

Do not speak negatively about your child's spouse to your child. This puts your child in an awkward position, and if he has to choose whom to support he must choose his wife. Remember their marriage is the priority relationship. This does not mean that you can't discuss things, but it must be done very carefully.

It's helpful if we don't distinguish between our child and our in-law child. I have five children but since they are all married I now have ten. Mentally and emotionally and in every other way I try to think of them equally and treat them in the same way. It's always a process.

5. Be quick to ask forgiveness and to grant grace.

We are going to blow it as in-laws a lot. It's important to say, "I shouldn't have said what I did (or done what I did) and I need to ask you to forgive me. Will you forgive me?" I've had to do this many times to all of my kids and my husband, but I've never felt like doing it. Often I'd rather say, "But you should have (or you shouldn't have) . . ." We go asking for forgiveness not because we feel like it but because we are commanded to. Feelings take time to heal and trust can take time to be restored, but this process cannot begin apart from going to one another and asking for forgiveness. We must assume the best, remember our kids are young, and strive to grant extra grace. And we have to recognize that God is much more patient with us than we are with ourselves. We never obtain a final degree in the school of parenting. We will always be learning!

Susan Alexander Yates, "How to Be a Great Mother-in-Law," *Susan Alexander Yates* (blog), originally published January 30, 2018, https://www.susanalexanderyates.com/great-mother-law/.

Susan Alexander Yates is the author of several books and is a regular guest on *FamilyLife Today* and other national radio programs. She and her husband, John, are popular speakers at marriage and parenting conferences and live in Virginia.

Connect with
Susan

VISIT
SUSANALEXANDERYATES.COM/COUSINCAMP
for Susan's blog, speaking events, and more!

 SUSANALEXANDERYATES